Major Muslim Nations

TUNISIA

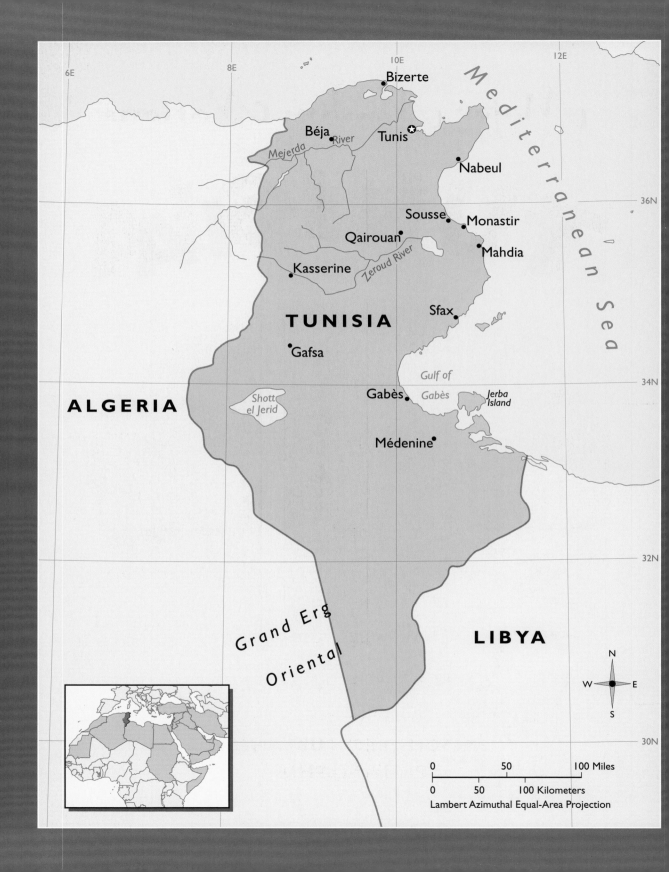

Bizerte

Béja

Mejerda   River   Tunis

Nabeul

36N

Sousse   Monastir

Qairouan   Mahdia

Kasserine   Zeroud River

TUNISIA

Sfax

Gafsa

34N

Gulf of

Shott
el Jerid   Gabès   Gabès   Jerba
Island

ALGERIA

Médenine

32N

LIBYA

Grand Erg

Oriental

N

W   E

S

30N

0   50   100 Miles

0   50   100 Kilometers

Lambert Azimuthal Equal-Area Projection

Major Muslim Nations

TUNISIA

ANNA CAREW-MILLER

MASON CREST PUBLISHERS
PHILADELPHIA

Mason Crest Publishers
370 Reed Road
Broomall, PA 19008
www.masoncrest.com

First printing

1 3 5 7 9 8 6 4 2

Library of Congress Cataloging-in-Publication Data

Carew-Miller, Anna.
  Tunisia / Anna Carew-Miller.
      p. cm. — (Major Muslim Nations)
  Includes index.
  ISBN 978-1-4222-1393-3 (hardcover) — ISBN 978-1-4222-1423-
7 (pbk.)
  1. Tunisia—Juvenile literature. I. Title.
  DT245.C354 2008
  961.1—dc22
                                        2008041228

Original ISBN: 1-59084-518-8 (hc)

Major Muslim Nations

TABLE OF CONTENTS

Major Muslim Nations

Dr. Harvey Sicherman, president and director of the Foreign Policy Research Institute, is the author of such books as *America the Vulnerable: Our Military Problems and How to Fix Them* (2002) and *Palestinian Autonomy, Self-Government and Peace* (1993).

Introduction

by Dr. Harvey Sicherman

America's triumph in the Cold War promised a new burst of peace and prosperity. Indeed, the decade between the demise of the Soviet Union and the destruction of September 11, 2001, seems in retrospect deceptively attractive. Today, of course, we are more fully aware—to our sorrow—of the dangers and troubles no longer just below the surface.

The Muslim identities of most of the terrorists at war with the United States have also provoked great interest in Islam and the role of religion in politics. A truly global religion, Islam's tenets are held by hundreds of millions of people from every ethnic group, scattered across the globe. It is crucial for Americans not to assume that Osama bin Laden's ideas are identical to those of most Muslims, or, for that matter, that most Muslims are Arabs. Also, it is important for Americans to understand the "hot spots" in the Muslim world because many will make an impact on the United States.

A glance at the map establishes the extraordinary coverage of our authors. Every climate and terrain may be found and every form of human society, from the nomads of the Central Asian steppes and Arabian deserts to highly sophisticated cities such as Cairo and Singapore. Economies range from barter systems to stock exchanges, from oil-rich countries to the thriving semi-market powers, such as India, now on the march. Others have built wealth on service and shipping.

The Middle East and Central Asia are heavily armed and turbulent. Pakistan is a nuclear power, Iran threatens to become one, and Israel is assumed to possess a small arsenal. But in other places, such as Afghanistan and the Sudan, the horse and mule remain potent instruments of war. All have a rich history of conflict, domestic and international, old and new.

Governments include dictatorships, democracies, and hybrids without a name; centralized and decentralized administrations; and older patterns of tribal and clan associations. The region is a veritable encyclopedia of political expression.

Although such variety defies easy generalities, it is still possible to make several observations.

First, the regional geopolitics reflect the impact of empires and the struggles of post-imperial independence. While centuries-old history is often invoked, the truth is that the modern Middle East political system dates only from the 1920s, when the Ottoman Empire dissolved in the wake of its defeat by Britain and France in World War I. States such as Algeria, Iraq, Israel, Jordan, Kuwait, Saudi Arabia, Syria, Turkey, and the United Arab Emirates did not exist before 1914—they became independent between 1920 and 1971. Others, such as Egypt and Iran, were dominated by foreign powers until well after World War II. Few of the leaders of these states were happy with the territories they were assigned or the borders, which were often drawn by Europeans. Yet the system has endured despite many efforts to change it.

A similar story may be told in South Asia. The British Raj dissolved into India and Pakistan in 1947. Still further east, Malaysia shares a British experience but Indonesia, a Dutch invention, has its own European heritage. These imperial histories weigh heavily upon the politics of the region.

The second observation concerns economics, demography, and natural resources. These countries offer dramatic geographical contrasts: vast parched deserts and high mountains, some with year-round snow; stone-hard volcanic rifts and lush semi-tropical valleys; extremely dry and extremely wet conditions, sometimes separated by only a few miles; large permanent rivers and wadis, riverbeds dry as a bone until winter rains send torrents of flood from the mountains to the sea.

Although famous historically for its exports of grains, fabrics, and spices, most recently the Muslim regions are known more for a single commodity: oil. Petroleum is unevenly distributed; while it is largely concentrated in the Persian Gulf and Arabian Peninsula, large oil fields can be found in Algeria, Libya, and further east in Indonesia. Natural gas is also abundant in the Gulf, and there are new, potentially lucrative offshore gas fields in the Eastern Mediterranean.

This uneven distribution of wealth has been compounded by demographics. Birth rates are very high, but the countries with the most oil are often lightly populated. Over the last decade, a youth "bulge" has emerged and this, combined with increased urbanization, has strained water supplies, air quality, public sanitation, and health services throughout the Muslim world. How will these young people be educated? Where will they work? A large outward migration, especially to Europe, indicates the lack of opportunity at home.

In the face of these challenges, the traditional state-dominated economic strategies have given way partly to experiments with "privatization" and foreign investment. But economic progress has come slowly, if at all, and most people have yet to benefit from "globalization," although there are pockets of prosperity, high technology (notably in Israel), and valuable natural resources (oil, gas, and minerals). Rising expectations have yet to be met.

A third important observation is the role of religion in the Middle East. Americans, who take separation of church and state for granted, should know that most countries in the region either proclaim their countries to be Muslim or allow a very large role for that religion in public life. (Islamic law, Sharia, permits people to practice Judaism and Christianity in Muslim states but only as *dhimmi*, "protected" but second-class citizens.) Among those with predominantly Muslim populations, Turkey alone describes itself as secular and prohibits avowedly religious parties in the political system. Lebanon was a Christian-dominated state, and Israel continues to be a Jewish state. Even where politics are secular, religion plays an enormous role in culture, daily life, and legislation.

Islam has deeply affected every state and people in these regions. But Islamic practices and groups vary from the well-known Sunni and Shiite groups to energetic Salafi (Wahhabi) and Sufi movements. Over the last 20 years especially, South and Central Asia have become battlegrounds for competing Shiite (Iranian) and Wahhabi (Saudi) doctrines, well financed from abroad and aggressively antagonistic toward non-Muslims and each other. Resistance to the Soviet war in Afghanistan brought these groups battle-tested warriors and organizers responsive to the doctrines made popular by Osama bin Laden and others. This newly significant struggle within Islam, superimposed on an older Muslim history, will shape political and economic destinies throughout the region and beyond.

We hope that these books will enlighten both teacher and student about the critical "hot spots" of the Muslim world. These countries would be important in their own right to Americans; arguably, after 9/11, they became vital to our national security. And the enduring impact of Islam is a crucial factor we must understand. We at the Foreign Policy Research Institute hope these books will illuminate both the facts and the prospects.

A colorful door is set into an ornate tile wall, Tunis.

Place in the World

Situated in North Africa, jutting into the Mediterranean Sea, is a small country with a long history and a peaceful culture known for its adaptability. Unlike the boundaries of many other countries in the Arab world, Tunisia's borders were not arbitrarily drawn in the 20th century by **Western** powers. Instead, its boundaries roughly follow the natural divisions of the Atlas Mountains in the west, the Mediterranean Sea in the north and east, and the Sahara Desert in the south. As a result, the idea of Tunisia and a distinct Tunisian culture has existed for centuries.

Although Tunisia is part of the Arab League and is a predominantly Muslim country, it also has strong ties to the Mediterranean world, to Africa, and to Europe. The country's name comes from Tunis, once an ancient **Phoenician** settlement and since the 1200s a capital city. Tunisia is inhabited by a people who can trace their roots to the Berber tribes that once dominated this land, to the Arab warriors who swept across North Africa in the seventh century, and to the Mediterranean peoples who traded with and, on occasion, conquered the land of Tunisia.

INFLUENCES ANCIENT AND MODERN

In ancient times, Tunisia was divided into two distinct areas—the coastal region and the inland region. The coast, with its fine harbors along Mediterranean trade routes, attracted one of the earliest seagoing civilizations, the Phoenicians. From their home city of Tyre, in what is now Lebanon, they explored the entire Mediterranean Sea. They built the city of Carthage, northeast of modern Tunis, as part of their great network of North African coastal cities. The Phoenicians traded with the natives of Tunisia, the Berbers. Intermarriage brought a blending of the two cultures.

Inland, the **Berber** tribes, possessing a distinct language and culture that evolved from prehistoric intermingling of peoples, dominated the land. Originally, they lived in tribal groups spread throughout North Africa. Some tribes lived in agricultural villages, while others were **nomadic** herders. Berber tribes still live in the Atlas Mountain regions of Morocco and Algeria. In Tunisia, the Berber people have blended with waves of immigrants who have settled there, and today only a handful of Berber communities still exist in the country.

The Phoenicians were not the only outsiders to covet the rich farmlands and safe ports of Tunisia. The Romans conquered Tunisia in the second century B.C., and the Byzantine Empire took control 600 years later. The grains and olive oil of Tunisia were traded throughout these empires. But the people of this region had a way of absorbing the culture of their conquerors without losing the qualities that made their own culture unique.

When the Islamic armies spread throughout North Africa beginning in the latter part of the seventh century A.D., the Berbers of the inland region and the coastal communities initially resisted the new religion. But they had in common with these strangers a lifestyle adapted to the desert environment, and they gradually accepted Islam. Muslim warriors mingled with the local populations wherever they spread Islam, and people of Arabic origin can be found from Morocco to Iran. Most modern Tunisians claim Arabic ancestry and speak Arabic.

Islamic empires controlled the political landscape of Tunisia for a millennium. The last such empire before the era of European domination was that of the Ottoman Turks.

In the mid-19th century the French took control of Tunisia. France, like other European powers of the time, claimed territories in Africa in large part to gain access to natural resources. The French had a great impact on modern Tunisia, shaping many of its institutions and heavily influencing its culture. Tunisian aspirations for independence were finally realized after World War II.

BOURGUIBA AND BEYOND

Many people give former president Habib Bourguiba much of the credit for shaping modern Tunisia. Bourguiba guided Tunisia through its transition from colonial state to independent nation, then served as the country's head for 31 years. A strong, idealistic leader who took pains to prevent government corruption, he championed the cause of social justice and, through the careful allocation of resources, charted a course toward economic development. By keeping his nation out of international conflicts, he both avoided the necessity of large military expenditures and minimized the armed forces' influence in Tunisian politics.

Under Bourguiba's rule, Tunisia became a moderate Arab state. Internationally, its policies were generally pro-Western.

Domestically, Bourguiba attempted to reduce the influence of Islam in Tunisian society. The consequences of that effort are particularly visible in the area of gender roles. By tradition, Islam has relegated women to an undeniably second-class status: their educational and work opportunities are generally limited, and Muslim men enjoy legally mandated superiority within the institution of marriage. However, beginning with the constitution written at the country's independence, Tunisian law moved toward greater equality between the sexes. Polygamy, or the practice of having multiple spouses at one time—which in Muslim cultures has been a prerogative of men only—was made illegal. In addition, the law made it easier for women to seek divorce, which had also been the sole right of men. Tunisian women became better educated and joined the workforce. In fact, Tunisia's urban middle-class women are among the most

Habib Bourguiba (1903–2000) is carried by supporters through the streets of Carthage, October 1987. After leading Tunisia to independence from France in 1956, Bourguiba ruled the country until being forced from office in 1987 by his prime minister, Ben Ali. The policies of Bourguiba shaped modern Tunisia.

emancipated in the Islamic world today.

But such changes did not occur without significant debate—and modernization has not come without problems. Beginning in the 1970s, for example, a growing gap between the rich and the poor created social unrest in Tunisia. Young people looked to the order of traditional Islam to restore their sense of importance in the world. **Islamist** political parties agitated for change and for a larger role in the political process. For its part, the government did not tolerate dissent: Tunisia developed an unfortunate record of limiting free speech and abusing the rights of political prisoners.

In 1987, after years of poor health, Bourguiba was removed from power by his prime minister, Zine El Abidine Ben Ali. It has been the task of Ben Ali to deal with the two greatest challenges facing modern Tunisia: fashioning a vibrant economy that benefits the poor as well as the rich and allowing more diverse points of view to shape the politics of the country. While the government has been quick to recognize problems in economic policy and correct them, it moves slowly, at best, toward democracy. The challenges of creating a truly democratic society continue to face the Tunisian people.

Like Muslim peoples throughout the Middle East and the **Maghreb**—the area of northwest Africa that includes Morocco, Algeria, Tunisia, and, some would say, part of Libya—Tunisians live with two competing cultures: the culture of the West, learned through colonialism and defined as modern, and their Arabic heritage, which for hundreds of years produced great cultural achievements but which was denigrated as inferior during colonial times. Tunisians are unified by a strong sense of ethnic identity and cultural pride, however, and their society is arguably more pragmatic than that of many Muslim neighbors. In contemporary Tunisia the values of order, stability, and enterprise are prominent, and many of its citizens seem determined to balance their traditional Arab heritage with the demands of modernization.

A *chott* is a salt lake that is dry during the summer but holds some water during the rainy winter season. The photo on the opposite page shows Chott el Jerid, the largest of these lakes, with piles of salt along its edges. At one time Chott el Jerid was part of the Mediterranean Sea. Today a causeway has been built across the *chott* so that people can travel from Kebili to Tozeur.

The Land

*T*unisia, which includes the northernmost tip of Africa, is situated in three different geographic regions: Africa, the Maghreb, and the Mediterranean. Tunisia's borders are formed, for the most part, by natural features of the landscape: the Atlas Mountains to the west, the Mediterranean Sea to the north and east, and the Sahara Desert to the south. Not only are its neighbors—Algeria to the west and Libya to the east—much larger, but Tunisia is one of the smallest countries on the African continent.

With a coastline of about 713 miles (1,148 kilometers), Tunisia is close to several important Mediterranean islands: Sardinia and Corsica to the north, Malta and Sicily to the northeast. In fact, Sicily lies a scant 100 miles (161 km) from Bizerte, Tunisia's northernmost port. For thousands of years, Tunisian merchants have traded with their European neighbors to the north, sharing many aspects of their culture.

The term *Maghreb*, which comes from an Arabic word meaning "the land of the setting sun," today refers to Morocco, Algeria, and Tunisia (and sometimes Libya). The countries of the Maghreb are linked by a common culture that blends Berber and Arab traditions. They also share two important geographical links: the Atlas Mountains and the Sahara Desert. The Atlas range begins in southwestern Morocco, extends through the north of Algeria, and ends in northeastern Tunisia. The Sahara Desert forms the southern border of the countries of the Maghreb, isolating North Africa from the vast continent to the south. In terms of geography and climate, Tunisia and the rest of North Africa have more in common with the Mediterranean world than with the rest of Africa.

THE MOUNTAINOUS NORTH

Two mountain chains run through northern Tunisia from southwest to northeast, ending not far from the Gulf of Tunis. These mountains, in Tunisia called the Northern Tell and High Tell Atlas, form the most prominent geographical feature of the country's northern region.

The Northern Tell, which roughly parallels the Mediterranean coast, is the lower of the two ranges. Its elevations rarely exceed about 3,000 feet (915 meters). Farther south, the more rugged High Tell—an extension of the Saharan Atlas Mountains of Algeria—contains Tunisia's highest peak. Jebel ech Chambi (Mount Chambi) rises 5,066 feet (1,544 meters).

Annual rainfall in the mountains may reach 40 inches (102 centimeters), and snow is occasionally seen at the higher elevations. Dense forests of cork oak and evergreen abound on the mountain slopes, particularly in more remote areas. At lower elevations, however, significant deforestation has occurred.

Separating the Northern Tell from the High Tell range is the Mejerda River. The Mejerda, which rises to the west in Algeria, flows northeast into the Gulf of Tunis. It is the only major river in Tunisia. The wide, fertile Mejerda River valley, a major agricultural region, is known for its grain and livestock production.

THE COASTAL PLAINS

Tunisia's eastern Mediterranean coast, from the Gulf of Tunis in the north to the Gulf of Gabès in the south, boasts fine harbors, sandy beaches, and many of the country's most important cities and towns. Extending inland from the Mediterranean throughout much of this area are coastal plains that contain a significant portion of Tunisia's limited fertile land. In the northeast part of the country, fruits and vegetables, especially citrus fruits, are widely grown. Cape Bon, which juts out into the Mediterranean, is famous for its wine-producing grapes.

This region of Tunisia has a typical Mediterranean climate, with hot, dry summers from June to August and mild, wet winters from December to February. Tunis, the country's capital and largest city, experiences high temperatures of around 90°F (32°C) and low

Lighthouses on jetties at Sidi Daoud, a fishing and canning center on the coast.

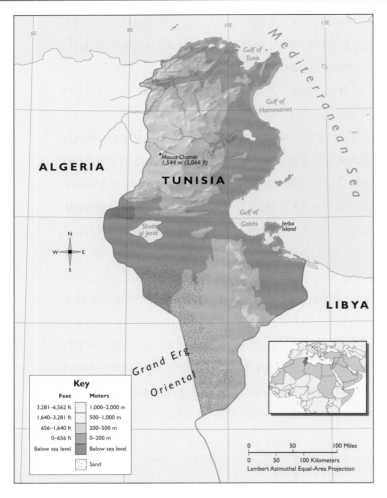

Tunisia's geography varies. The fertile, low-lying area along the Mediterranean coast includes much of the country's arable land. Mountains run through the northwest and south, and a plateau runs through central Tunisia. Chott Djerid (Shott el Jerid), a large salt lake, is also located in the central region. To the south lies the Sahara, the world's largest desert.

temperatures of around 40°F (4°C). Average annual rainfall is about 22.5 inches (57.2 centimeters).

Farther south, between the Gulf of Hammamet and the Gulf of Gabès, the irregular coastline features wide beaches and good harbors, such as those of the ancient cities of Sousse and Sfax. Inland the humid coastal plain and low hills of this central part of Tunisia form the **Sahel**, one of the country's most important regions. Although it makes up only 20 percent of Tunisia's total land area, the Sahel is home to nearly half of the country's population.

Ancient villages and groves of olive, pomegranate, and almond trees dot the landscape. The history of the Sahel reaches back into antiquity, when the region's olive groves supplied the Roman Empire with olive oil. At El Djem, the ruins of a Roman amphitheater constitute one of the most important archaeological sites in North Africa. The history of the region and its fine beaches make the towns of Sousse and Monastir popular with tourists.

Just off the coast from the city of Sfax are the Kerkennah Islands, made up of two larger islands, Chargui and Gharbi, as well as several uninhabited islets. Covered in palm trees and vineyards and surrounded by many quiet lagoons, the islands are popular tourist destinations.

THE CENTRAL PLATEAU

In central Tunisia, between the coastal plains in the east and the High Tell Mountains in the north and west, lies a wide plateau—an expanse of relatively flat land at elevation. Dry and hot, the plateau is divided roughly in half into the higher western section (sometimes called the High Steppe) and the lower eastern section (the Low Steppe). The western half is composed largely of broad basins and occasional low peaks; gravel covers large portions of the eastern half.

Throughout the plateau, where rainfall is unreliable, the vegetation is comparatively sparse, consisting mainly of scrub bushes. However, at the far southeast corner of the plateau lies Bou Hedma National Park, home to Tunisia's last remnant of pre-Saharan savanna. This

The olive tree suits Tunisia's climate perfectly because it can survive long periods of drought. Ranging in height from 10 to 40 feet (3 to 12 meters), olive trees can live for hundreds of years because their wood resists decay so well. Olive oil was once an essential ingredient for making soap; today it is used primarily for cooking and processing food.

type of grassland once blanketed the non-mountainous regions of northern Africa, but over the last few millennia the Sahara Desert has slowly expanded northward.

Central Tunisia, including the plateau region, was traditionally the home of nomadic herders, whose lifestyle stood in stark contrast to that of the settled peoples who inhabited the coastal ports and farming villages. Even today there are few urban centers in this region. One exception is the holy city of Kairouan (also spelled Qairouan), which sits near the eastern edge of the central plateau. Islamic armies established Kairouan in the late seventh century as they conquered North Africa. Kairouan was also at the crossroads of the ancient camel caravan routes, which crossed the Sahara to reach the Arab world farther east.

The forests near Aïn Draham, in the north near the border with Algeria, are unusual for a North African country.

THE BARREN SOUTH

South of the central plateau, Tunisia's climate becomes progressively hotter and drier, and the land more barren. At the northern edge of this area, modest rainfall during the winter months fills depressions to create shallow, temporary salt lakes (called *chotts* or *shotts*), which dry up as the water evaporates during the summer months. Three large *chotts* lie in this region. The largest is Chott Djerid (also spelled Shott el Jerid); Chott el-Gharsa (or Shott al Gharsah) contains Tunisia's lowest point, at 56 feet (17 meters) below sea level.

Farther south, Tunisia is shaped like an inverted triangle with its base stretching from the Algerian border in the west to the Mediterranean border with Libya in the east. Here the land gives way to the Sahara Desert, parts of which may receive no rainfall for years on end. Outside of the occasional oasis—a fertile area supplied by a reliable underground source of water—no permanent vegetation exists and only a few nomads cross the land. Within the oasis communities, residents depend heavily on their date palm trees.

WILDLIFE AND ENVIRONMENTAL ISSUES

Tunisia's wildlife has suffered from centuries of pressure from human populations, though the government has in recent years undertaken conservation efforts. The Barbary deer and a few species of gazelle, once near extinction from hunting, are now protected. Other endangered species have been reintroduced into Bou Hedma National Park. These include two antelope species, the addax and the oryx, as well as ostriches and the maned mouflon, a species of wild sheep.

The forests of the north are home to a variety of animals, from wild boar and mongoose to porcupines and genets, tree-climbing carnivores in the feline family. In the south, wildlife includes mammals such as gerbils, foxes, hares, and the suslik, a kind of rodent. An unusual lizard, the desert varanid, which is related to Indonesia's Komodo dragon, shares the desert with horned vipers and scorpions.

Tunisia is located along the migratory routes of various bird species, making it a popular destination for bird-watchers. Migrating storks, hawks, and eagles make an appearance in the spring. In the fall, Tunisia hosts a variety of wading birds and waterfowl. Ichkeul National Park in the north is a sanctuary for water birds of all types.

Tunisia faces a number of environmental problems, some of which are related to the dry climate. The mountainous northern

The Geography of Tunisia

Location: northern Africa, bordering the Mediterranean Sea, between Libya and Algeria

Area: slightly smaller than Georgia and Connecticut combined
   total: 63,170 square miles (163,610 sq km)
   land: 59,984 square miles (155,360 sq km)
   water: 3,185 square miles (8,250 sq km)

Borders: Algeria, 600 miles (965 km); Libya, 285 miles (459 km)

Climate: temperate, with mild winters and hot summers in the north; desert in the south

Terrain: mountains in the north; hot, dry central plain; semiarid south merges with the Sahara Desert

Elevation extremes:
   lowest point: Chott el-Gharsa (Shott al Gharsah): 56 feet (17 meters) below sea level
   highest point: Jebel ech Chambi (Mount Chambi): 5,066 feet (1,544 meters)

Natural hazards: none

Source: Adapted from CIA World Factbook, 2008.

An oasis in the Tunisian mountains near Tamerza. Like the other countries of North Africa, much of Tunisia's geography combines mountains and desert areas.

region is the only part of the country that receives reliable rainfall, and the Mejerda River is the only river certain not to run dry. Having enough drinkable water can be a problem, especially during the summer. All water resources are controlled by the Ministry of Agriculture, which carefully plans the building of dams, the development of irrigation projects, and the drilling of wells.

A little less than 20 percent of Tunisia's land is arable—that is, suitable for growing crops. And human activity, such as the clearing of woodlands, overgrazing of livestock, and poor farming techniques, have combined with natural conditions, including strong winds and blowing sand, to make soil erosion a serious concern. Tunisia's government has attempted to address the problem by instituting reforestation programs and teaching farmers soil conservation techniques.

Little remains of the ancient Punic port at Carthage, which was once one of the most important in the Mediterranean world. The term *Punic*, which refers to the seafaring Carthaginian civilization that was centered in modern-day Tunisia, comes from the Latin word *Poeni* ("Phoenicians"). Phoenicians from the eastern Mediterranean established Carthage as a trading post late in the ninth century B.C.

History

The history of human culture in Tunisia goes back thousands of years. Early farming methods reached the Nile Valley from the Fertile Crescent region in about 5000 B.C. From there, farming spread to the Maghreb by about 4000 B.C. The humid coastal plains of central Tunisia were home to early agricultural communities, populated by the ancestors of the Berber tribes. They lived in both settled villages and nomadic tribal groups.

PHOENICIAN INFLUENCES

Around the 12th century B.C., Phoenician traders from the region that is now Lebanon began settling the Tunisian coast. The Phoenicians spread their colonies along the North African coast, with the goal of controlling trade in the western Mediterranean Sea. The Phoenicians arrived concurrent with a global climate change that caused the Sahara Desert to grow larger, and communication with the African continent to the south became more difficult. From that time onward, human culture in Tunisia was strongly oriented toward the coast.

One of the most powerful colonies was the city-state of Carthage, which means "New City." Its traditional date of founding is 814 B.C. Along with other Phoenician colonial cities such as Utica, Carthage grew as wealthy and strong as the Phoenicians' home city of Tyre. Eventually, the city-states of Tunisia, led by Carthage, broke away from Tyre and established their own empire. Carthage and the other city-states are important to the history of the Maghreb

because they introduced intensive agriculture, metalworking, and writing to this region of the African continent.

Few records from the Phoenicians survive, but it is believed that the colonists stayed on the coast until the sixth century B.C. Tunis, Bizerte, Sousse, Monastir, and Sfax began as trading posts where the Phoenician merchants traded with the Berbers of the interior. When the colonists pushed into the interior, they extended the territory of Carthage into the fertile plains of northern and eastern Tunisia.

A division between the cities and farming communities on the coast and the nomadic herdsmen in the interior is typical of the history of North Africa west of Egypt. The Berbers on the coast adapted to the Phoenician culture, even adopting the Semitic language of the Phoenician seamen. In the northern coastal plains, the Carthaginians established large wheat farms. In the Sahel region along the eastern coast, they planted olive groves, for which the region is still well known. In the interior, Berber tribal kingdoms

(Opposite) While excavating in Carthage, American archaeologists discovered this cemetery where, most scientists believe, the remains of children who had been ritually sacrificed were buried. It is estimated that the incinerated remains of at least 20,000 children were buried here between 400 and 200 B.C.

The Phoenician practice of child sacrifice to their god Baal Hamon was noted by many ancient writers. In fact, the name of this cemetery, Tophet, comes from references in the Bible to places where the Phoenicians performed their sacrifices. In the third century B.C., the Greek author Kleitarchos wrote, "Out of reverence for Kronos [the Greek name for Baal Hamon], the Phoenicians, and especially the Carthaginians, whenever they seek to obtain some great favor, vow one of their children, burning it as a sacrifice to the deity, if they are especially eager to gain success. There stands in their midst a bronze statue of Kronos, its hands extended over a bronze brazier, the flames of which engulf the child. When the flames fall on the body, the limbs contract and the open mouth seems almost to be laughing, until the contracted body slips quietly into the brazier."

This Carthaginian pendant made of sand-core glass was created in the fourth or third century B.C. Beautiful artworks such as this one emerged from the culture of Carthage; the city also produced a democratic system of government in which leaders were selected by the people. In 340 B.C. the Greek philosopher Aristotle praised the constitution of Carthage.

controlled the land and the farming and nomadic communities that lived there.

THE ROMAN ERA

In 241 B.C., Carthage lost its first war with Rome, a rising power in the Mediterranean. In the aftermath, Carthaginian rulers attempted to establish greater control over the Berbers in the surrounding area through taxes and forced labor. One Berber chieftain, Masinissa, joined Rome to help defeat the Carthaginians in 202 B.C.

Carthage was completely destroyed by Rome in 146 B.C., and the site remained deserted for 100 years before being rebuilt as an administrative center for the Roman Empire in Africa. Large-scale

Roman colonization throughout North Africa began in the first century B.C. By the early first century A.D., there were more than 10,000 Roman immigrants in this region, which had become Rome's most important source of grain. Over the next three centuries, Tunisia became Rome's chief supplier of olive oil. The region was peaceful and prosperous, with thriving towns that had forums, markets, public entertainments, and baths. Most of the population consisted of Berber farmers.

Roman power was centered in the coastal towns, while great agricultural estates or villas existed in the interior. Roman villas and Berber villages existed side by side, with the number of villages increasing toward the southern portion of Tunisia. Often, powerful

The ruins of a Roman village built near the site of ancient Carthage. Though the Romans razed the city at the end of the Third Punic War in 146 B.C., by A.D. 37 a new Roman city had been built on the same site. The Roman destruction of the original Carthage was so complete that little remains from the Punic civilization.

Berber families adopted Roman culture and lifestyles. Over the centuries, this pattern of adaptability to the culture of conquerors would be characteristic of the Berbers.

By the beginning of the third century, Roman control over Tunisia began to weaken. Coastal towns continued to thrive, often as centers of Christianity, but the inland estates began to break up. Tribal herders of the interior became more powerful in large part because of the arrival of an animal first domesticated in Arabia: the camel. This hardy animal, which can go without water for up to

A fort that dates from the rule of the Byzantine Empire overlooks the village of Kelibia. The Byzantines took control of the Tunisia area in the sixth century, after the fall of the Western Roman Empire. However, the Maghreb would slip from Byzantine control by the seventh century.

seven days, would radically change life in the desert. Berber farmers in the highlands of the north remained independent during this time.

Christianity seems to have reached this region by the second century. The first firm evidence is the record of the execution of 12 Christians in Carthage in A.D. 180 for refusing to sacrifice in honor of the Roman emperor. Many Berbers became Christian because it was a religion of protest and was consistent with Berber ideals of honor and independence.

Roman control of Tunisia ended when the Vandals, a warlike Germanic tribe, swept across Europe through Spain and landed in Morocco in 429. They took Carthage in 439 as they extended their power across North Africa. In the sixth century, the Vandals were defeated by the Eastern Roman, or Byzantine, Empire (in the late fourth century the Roman Empire had been divided into eastern and western halves). Thereafter Tunisia became part of the Byzantine Empire, which was centered in Constantinople (the site of modern-day Istanbul, Turkey). But archaeological evidence shows that the area continued to decline during the Byzantine era. Cities and agricultural areas shrunk as tribes of nomadic Berber herdsmen became more powerful.

THE COMING OF ISLAM

Arabs—inspired by their new religion, Islam—began their conquest of North Africa in 639, when the army of Amir ibn al-As invaded Egypt. The Muslim army moved into Libya by 643, and in 647, it defeated Byzantine forces near the modern city of Sbeïtla in Tunisia.

Around 670, a Muslim general founded the city of Kairouan in the central inland region and made it the capital of the new Muslim province of Ifriqiya. Soon afterward, the Islamic armies were nearly wiped out by Berber forces, which restricted Arab power to the region around Kairouan. The Arabs regarded the Berbers as barbarians, and many Berbers saw the Arabs as oppressive tax collectors. This hostility slowed the conversion of the Berber population to Islam.

Over the following decades, however, the Berbers did convert to Islam in large numbers. By 705 the Maghreb was an integral part of the Islamic world. The Islamic army that invaded Spain in 710 was composed largely of Berber warriors, although estimates suggest that as little as 10 percent of the Berber population had converted by this time.

The Arabs formed an urban *elite*, controlling the coastal cities and towns, as well as Kairouan. The Berbers continued to live in small farming villages and in nomadic tribes of herders.

A succession of Muslim rulers began with the Umayyad *caliphs*, who ruled the Islamic empire from Damascus, in present-day Syria, until 750. The Maghreb was difficult to rule from this distance, but the Umayyads did not consider the region important. The successors to the Umayyad Caliphate, the Abbasids, moved the capital of their empire to Baghdad, in present-day Iraq, which had the effect of making North Africa more independent.

The Berbers did not assimilate entirely, or always smoothly, into Arab culture. At first, they preserved their own language, in different dialects, and they frequently interpreted Islam according to their own ideals. But over time, the cultural influence of the Arab Muslim world was significant. Where Islam came, the Arabic language slowly spread. Mosques and *madrasas*, schools for teaching Islam, were built in the architectural style of the East.

In 800 an Arab governor established the Aghlabid dynasty in Kairouan, basically making the region independent of the caliphate in Baghdad. By this time, the majority of the population was Muslim, especially the urban and settled communities. The blending of Arab and Berber peoples formed a distinct Tunisian cultural and political identity. Kairouan became a center of spiritual and intellectual life in the Maghreb.

In 910 a new Islamic dynasty came to power and moved the capital to a Tunisian coastal fortress named Mahdia. The armies of the Fatimids soon took over Egypt, establishing their capital in Cairo. By the 11th century, the Berber governors of Kairouan declared their independence from Cairo and established the Zirid dynasty.

This dynasty was threatened by the arrival of the Banu Hilal, a nomadic Arab tribe from the east, who destroyed Kairouan in 1057. Less warlike than the Banu Hilal tribe, the Zirid rulers moved to the coast. Tunis became the capital city, and Kairouan never regained

This page from a 12th-century Arabic manuscript shows a caravan passing a fortified town. The Arabs had conquered most of the coastal areas of North Africa by the end of the seventh century, although the Berbers in the interior would maintain their independence for several hundred years. The Tunisia area was ruled by a succession of Islamic Arab dynasties until the 13th century.

its former glory. Inland, the Berber farmers moved to mountain villages, and the plains of Tunisia became more Arabic in culture. Eventually the dominant language shifted from Berber to Arabic.

The weak Zirid regime fell in 1160 to the Almohads. This new Berber dynasty was founded in southern Morocco by a pious scholar preaching moral reform and strict piety. The Almohads quickly united much of the Maghreb and parts of Spain under their rule. Christianity nearly disappeared from the region of Tunisia during this time. Under the Almohad dynasty, a new culture, called **Moorish**, emerged from its territories in Spain and North Africa. This culture produced distinctive forms of art, architecture, and literature.

With the decline of Almohad power in the 13th century, much of Tunisia came under the control of Berber Hafsid caliphs, who ruled from about 1230 to 1574. Their power was centered in the northern cities of Tunisia and relied on **mercenary** armies. They paid for their armies by trading with Europeans, who by this time had begun to control much of the commerce in the Mediterranean region. Along the trade routes, Spanish silk, gold from western Africa, metals, and olive oil were important. By the 15th century Spain had become the most powerful European regime in the region and threatened Muslim control in the Maghreb. European pirates in the eastern Mediterranean also posed problems.

In the Maghreb three Islamic dynasties ruled: the Hafsids in Tunisia, the Ziyanids in Algeria, and the Marinids in Morocco. The boundaries of their empires were not clearly drawn but corresponded roughly with the national boundaries of these countries today. Control of each region radiated from cities, and in the plateau or desert country, a ruler's main interest lay in keeping trade routes open. In certain areas tribal chiefs were granted control in exchange for military service.

During the Hafsid era, Tunisia developed its distinctive culture

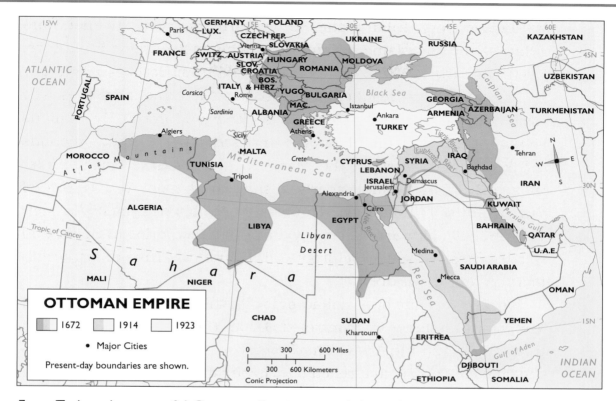

From Turkey, the powerful Ottoman Empire spread throughout the Middle East during the 15th and 16th centuries. By 1672 the empire controlled large parts of North Africa, as well as much of the rest of the Middle East, central Asia, and eastern Europe. By the start of World War I (1914), however, the Ottomans had been forced out of North Africa, and the French controlled the Tunisian region.

and identity in the Muslim world. Tunisian craftsmen, merchants, and farmers thrived in the largely peaceful coastal communities. Inland, nomadic Arab tribes dominated. The power of the Hafsids, centered in Tunis, was weakened by the bubonic plague. Known as the Black Death in Europe, this disease reached the Maghreb in 1348 through Sicily, decimating the population.

THE OTTOMAN PERIOD

In 1574 Tunis was conquered by the Ottoman Empire and was made a provincial capital of this part of North Africa. The

This charcoal and watercolor depiction of Europeans and Turks fighting in Tunisia shows Emperor Charles V (1500–1558) at the head of the Holy Roman Empire's cavalry. In 1535 Charles led a successful attack against the Turkish-supported pirate Barbarossa (1465–1546), who had founded the kingdom of Algiers (in Tunisia's modern-day neighbor Algeria) and had directed raids against European shipping in the Mediterranean. Despite the success of Charles's attack, pirate raids from the Barbary Coast (as Europeans called the coastal area of modern-day Morocco, Algeria, Tunisia, and Libya) would continue until the 19th century.

Ottomans—Muslims, but Turks rather than Arabs—divided their holdings into *vilayets* (provinces) ruled by *pashas* (governors). In part because of the distance between Tunis and Istanbul, the seat of the Ottoman Empire, an Arabic Ottoman culture developed in Tunisia. The influence of the Turkish culture and language of the Ottomans extended only to the coastal regions, and Arabic remained the dominant language of government.

At first, the provincial government included a pasha sent from Istanbul, an administration of locals, a professional army made up of elite Turkish soldiers called janissaries, and a navy. The Ottomans used Tunis and other North African ports as naval bases from which to check Spanish expansion.

Tunisian society during the Ottoman era was highly stratified. In the cities, the military noblemen, called **notables**, and the merchants formed the upper rank; below them stood tradesmen and craftsmen; and below them, laborers and slaves. In the countryside, most residents were peasants and small farmers who controlled their own land, supporting the ruling class through the payment of taxes. Relatively prosperous farmers cultivated olives in the Sahel; poor sharecroppers worked on estates in the north. Far inland, nomadic herdsmen paid taxes only when forced to by military expeditions.

By the 17th century the Ottoman Empire had entered a long period of decline under the pressures of internal corruption, a series of costly wars, and the rise of the European powers (though the empire's complete dissolution would come only with World War I). In North Africa the decline of Ottoman power translated into greater local control. Authorities in Tunis functioned more and more like independent governments rather than representatives of the sultan, as the Ottoman Empire's ruler was called.

By 1705 Tunisia was nearly independent of the Ottoman Empire in all but name. A dynasty founded by a local military commander called a **bey** actually controlled the government. The bey balanced the interests of the Arab urban elite with the demands of the Ottoman court. Under this arrangement the region experienced a good degree of prosperity throughout the 18th century.

By the 19th century, however, European trading corporations had gained control of much of the economic activity in the Middle East and North Africa, including Tunisia. Trade with Europe tended to be imbalanced: Tunisia supplied cheaper raw materials, such as olive oil for making soap, in exchange for more expensive manufactured goods from Europe.

The European nations' hunger for raw materials fed their colonial ambitions in Africa. European powers competed with one another for dominance and used their military might to establish control over many African territories. The French invaded Tunisia's neighbor, Algeria, in the 1830s. After the defeat of the Algerians, many European colonials poured into the Maghreb. In response, the Ottomans increased their presence in Tripoli, in neighboring Libya, in 1835. But the French dominated the region economically.

Caught between the French colonial power to the west and the Ottomans to the east, Tunisia faced a very difficult period in the mid-19th century. Tunisia's ruler, Ahmed Bey (1837–55), tried to modernize his country. He promoted greater economic self-reliance. He adopted new legal codes modeled on those of Europe and abolished slavery so that European powers would not be able to use that institution as a pretext for intervening in Tunisian affairs. As a further deterrent, he attempted to create a large modern army. Heavy taxation on residents in the Tunisian countryside failed to generate sufficient revenue to fund the army, and Ahmed turned to France for loans, beginning a period of debt to the West. Worse, the plans for a modern army had to be scrapped.

The next Tunisian bey put in place a constitution, the first of its kind in the Muslim world. With European parliamentary governments as the model, the constitution called for a council of 60 members to approve certain laws; the bey promised to govern within the limits of these laws. These reforms had only limited success, perhaps because they were highly influenced by European advisers and did not emerge from the native culture. The ruling elite and the urban merchant class benefited most from the changes.

Increased taxes, which followed a period of bad harvests and epidemics, caused a revolt in 1864, which left the economy in a shambles. Further reforms attracted foreign investment to Tunisia, but they also opened the door to foreign governments, particularly

France. Forced to borrow from European sources to pay off loans to France, the government found that public debt was higher than its revenue by 1869.

TUNISIA UNDER THE FRENCH

Despite attempts to bring the Tunisian economy into the modern world, problems continued. In the meantime, Africa was being carved up by European powers with colonial interests, and Italy, coming late to this race for conquest, was interested in Tunisia. This situation, along with Tunisia's unpaid debts to Europeans, led to the establishment of a French **protectorate** in 1881.

Under French rule the infrastructure of Tunisia improved, as the French built roads and railroads. Unfortunately, only the upper levels of society benefited from this modernization. In the countryside, more and more peasants lost control of community land to private ownership. Increasingly, these owners were Frenchmen and other Europeans. The government of the protectorate favored these land transfers and encouraged settlement by Europeans, called **colons**.

Unlike some other European colonies, however, Tunisia largely retained its own culture. Except for members of the elite, Tunisians rarely interacted with the French. Compared with Algeria, there were fewer French *colons* actually living in Tunisia, even though the French had taken control of a great deal of Tunisian territory. By 1892 French *colons* and corporations owned one-fifth of the arable land in Tunisia, but 90 percent of that land was in the hands of just 16 large landowners.

The unbalanced economy of colonial trade continued, with less valuable raw materials being traded for more expensive manufactured goods from Europe. Before World War I, Tunisia was Europe's main supplier of phosphates. During this period, Tunisia experienced modest population growth. While the amount of cultivated land doubled, the number of people who did not own the land they worked also increased. Many Tunisians became sharecroppers; others migrated to cities, and Tunis experienced tremendous population growth during this time.

Colonial rule improved education for the elite. In addition to the traditional Islamic *madrasas*, there were now specialized schools for the training of public officials, military officers, doctors, and engineers in Tunis. Secondary schools, modeled on those found in France, were also established. Young men educated in these schools and in European universities began to demand a voice in the future of their country. In 1907 a group called the Young Tunisians demanded inclusion in the French political system and greater opportunities for education. At this stage, however, even militant Tunisians stopped short of calling for a withdrawal of the French from their country.

World War I (1914–18) led to the complete breakup of the Ottoman Empire. Even though Ottoman control in places like Tunisia had long been almost totally symbolic, the disappearance of the political structure that most Arabic-speaking lands had known for hundreds of years changed the way many Arabs thought about their place in the world. In Tunisia, ideas about self-determination began percolating. Tunisian soldiers, who had fought alongside the French on the western front, expected the right to participate fully in their country's political process.

The French had other ideas. They considered control of the Maghreb too important to their interests to cede power to locals. The region provided manpower for the French army and raw materials for French industry. Many French citizens lived there, considerable amounts of French money were tied up in investments there, and routes to French possessions in central Africa began there. After the war, the French government encouraged even more colonial settlement in Tunisia.

In response, Tunisians created the Destour (Constitution) Party. Urban and middle class in orientation, the party had few ties with farmers or laborers. Strictly speaking, the Destour Party was not a nationalist organization, for it merely sought to limit the powers of the bey (through whom the French controlled Tunisian politics), not to expel France from the country. Yet France remained unresponsive even to this limited goal.

For some educated young Tunisians, the goals and methods of the Destour Party were too moderate, and they founded the Neo-Destour Party in 1933. Led by Habib Bourguiba and others educated at French universities, this was Africa's first true nationalist party outside of Egypt. The Neo-Destour Party appealed not only to the educated elite but also to those who lived in farming towns and villages of the Sahel.

During the years Tunisia was a French protectorate, the nominal ruler of the country was a member of the Husainid family. This dynasty had gained power in Tunis and remained the hereditary rulers until Tunisia's independence in 1956. Sidi Ahmed II became the bey of Tunis in 1929; during his rule the Axis powers conquered France and fought for control of North Africa. After American, British, and Free French forces defeated the Germans in North Africa, Ahmed was accused of collaborating with the Nazis, forced to abdicate the thrown, and sent into exile.

During the 1930s the worldwide economic depression wreaked havoc on the Tunisian economy. Prices for agricultural and mining products—mainstays of the economy—plummeted. A drought caused further hardship. Many rural people were forced from their land. In increasing numbers they moved to cities, and many settled outside Tunis, Sfax, and Bizerte in squalid shantytowns. All of this made Tunisians more politically active. In 1938 nationalist-inspired rioting claimed the lives of 122 Tunisians.

World War II, which broke out the following year, would bring further hardships to Tunisia—and add to the momentum for political change. In 1940 Germany inflicted a shocking, humiliating, and total defeat on France; in 1942 the Germans invaded Tunisia. The Kasserine Pass, southwest of Tunis, was the scene of particularly bitter fighting between American and German forces. By May 1943, the Allied forces of Great Britain and the United States had compelled Germany to surrender its last stronghold in North Africa,

on Tunisia's Cape Bon. Throughout the campaign, Tunisian soldiers had fought with the Allies; they would also take part in the liberation of France in 1944.

THE MOVEMENT FOR SELF-DETERMINATION

At the end of the war in 1945, France tried to reestablish control of its overseas colonies, but it met with resistance. In Tunisia, nationalists increasingly demanded nothing less than self-determination. The Neo-Destour Party expanded its power base dramatically by attracting the support of well-organized trade unions. But the French agreed only to superficial reforms.

When Habib Bourguiba organized a civil disobedience campaign, the French government in Tunisia outlawed the Neo-Destour Party and threw Bourguiba into prison. In 1946 Bourguiba escaped to Cairo and later went to the United States, where he promoted the cause of Tunisian nationalism. When he returned to Tunisia in 1949, he was again imprisoned.

A turning point came when a new French government decided to negotiate with the Tunisian nationalists in 1950. In spite of opposition from French *colons*, Tunisia was given more autonomy. However, rural peasants—not satisfied with the slow transition toward full independence—formed armed groups and attacked French *colons* in the countryside. French troops could not stop the uprising. In 1954 Bourguiba was released from prison to negotiate the agreement that led to Tunisian independence.

(Opposite) Habib Bourguiba and his wife in exile, late 1940s. Bourguiba's efforts were instrumental in helping Tunisia achieve independence in 1956.

INDEPENDENCE AND THE BOURGUIBA YEARS

Thanks largely to the leadership of Habib Bourguiba, Tunisia achieved its independence in 1956—and did so with comparatively little bloodshed. Bourguiba was elected the nation's first prime minister, with the bey retaining certain powers. In 1957 Bourguiba deposed the bey and Tunisia became a republic; Bourguiba served as its president. The new government was controlled almost entirely by the Neo-Destour Party and affiliated trade unions.

Newly independent Tunisia faced many challenges. The economy had not fully recovered from the war and the earlier drought, and

French foreign minister Christian Pineau (right) and Tunisian premier Tahar Ben Ammar shake hands after signing an agreement on March 20, 1956, that guaranteed independence for Tunisia.

rural immigrants poured into the cities looking for work. Relations with France were tense; Algerian nationalists had launched a war for independence in 1954, and guerrilla units operated from Tunisian territory. Moreover, thousands of Algerian refugees had fled across the border into Tunisia.

As president, Bourguiba worked quickly to modernize his country, launching a host of social and economic reforms. In particular, he targeted Islamic religious regulations and customs that he believed prevented positive change. Religious courts were abolished and restrictive laws governing marriage and the rights of women were rewritten. But Bourguiba sometimes pushed for more reform than his fellow Tunisians would accept. In 1961, for example, he suggested that fasting during the Muslim holy month of Ramadan be abolished, as it hurt the economy of the country. The idea raised a storm of controversy among Tunisia's many devout Muslims and soon had to be abandoned.

Bourguiba's government focused on education as a long-term solution to the challenge of improving the country's standard of living. Between the end of World War II and 1960, the number of Tunisian children attending school increased by 50 percent. The need for an educated professional class of doctors, engineers, and lawyers also grew, so the government established the modern University of Tunis. In spite of these efforts, many young Tunisians migrated to France in order to find better economic opportunities during the 1950s and 1960s.

Economically, Bourguiba steered his country toward **socialism**, a system in which the government owns the means of production and manages the distribution of goods. The government controlled various sectors of the economy in an effort to encourage growth. Land reform was directed at reducing rural poverty. Large-scale irrigation projects were started to increase agricultural productivity. The government bought or seized land that had been owned by

Tunis hosted the offices of the Arab League, an organization of Arab states that had been formed in 1945, after Egyptian president Anwar Sadat (left) and Israel's prime minister Menachem Begin (right) signed a peace agreement that had been negotiated with the help of U.S. president Jimmy Carter. Tunis remained the home of the Arab League's headquarters from 1979 to 1989.

French *colons*, creating large, state-run farms. The government also took control of mining operations, especially phosphate mines, in an effort to increase productivity.

During the 1960s, the socialist, left-leaning, anti-Western president of Egypt, Gamal Abdel Nasser, had a great deal of influence throughout the Arab world. Nasser worked to destabilize pro-Western Arab governments in order to decrease the role of Western powers in the region and to promote his vision of Arab unity—under his leadership. Unlike other Arab nations, Tunisia was not significantly influenced by Nasser's politics because Bourguiba and the Neo-Destour Party had strong popular support. During this time, however, the government party was renamed the Destourian Socialist Party.

In foreign policy Bourguiba maintained an independent stance. Tunisia joined the Arab League in 1958, but Bourguiba broke with the Arab mainstream—and incurred the wrath of Nasser—by proposing recognition of Israel as part of an overall peace settlement. Further strains were created by the new economic direction Tunisia took in the 1970s. Concluding that the socialist policies of its state-controlled economy were failing, the government passed new laws designed to encourage free enterprise and investment. These laws fostered a strong relationship with the developed nations of the West, which made Tunisia more unpopular with some of its Arab neighbors.

In the late 1970s, however, the actions of Egypt's leader Anwar el-Sadat would help draw Tunisia closer to the mainstream of Arab politics. After Sadat negotiated a peace settlement with Israel in 1978–79, Egypt was expelled from the Arab League, and the organization's headquarters were moved from Cairo to Tunis (where they remained until 1989). In addition, Tunisia agreed to permit the Palestine Liberation Organization to establish its headquarters in Tunis when the Israeli army drove the PLO out of Lebanon in 1982. But Bourguiba was careful to restrict the PLO's contact with Tunisian citizens, and Tunisia continued to adopt a moderate stance on the Arab-Israeli conflict.

THE DECLINE OF BOURGUIBA'S POPULARITY

During the 1970s, popular support for Habib Bourguiba and the ruling party began to decline, and social and political unrest increased. Student demonstrations and labor strikes, fueled by unemployment and demands for higher pay, broke out. In 1978 at least 150 Tunisians were killed when strikers clashed with police and security forces. Claiming that labor leaders were attempting to start an uprising, the government arrested many of them.

The issue of Bourguiba's age (he was born in 1903) and his frequent health problems also became a concern, and Tunisians wondered how a successor for their longtime leader would be chosen. In 1975 Bourguiba was elected president-for-life, but the government approved a plan to have the prime minister automatically succeed him if Bourguiba died or became incapacitated by illness.

In the midst of the domestic conflict and uncertainty, a not inconsiderable portion of Tunisia's population turned to the teachings of Islamic fundamentalists for guidance and solace. By the early 1980s, Islamists—Muslims who wanted a conservative interpretation of Islam to be the basis of government and society—had begun to have influence on politics throughout the Arab world. In Tunisia the most important of these groups was the Islamic Tendency Movement (MTI). Led mostly by university students, the MTI advocated returning to a moral society governed by Islamic law, a message that appealed to the urban poor. Bourguiba's strategy for dealing with the Islamists was to jail them for treason.

But others besides the MTI were agitating for change. In response to widespread demands for a more democratic government, Bourguiba allowed a few political parties besides the ruling Destourian Socialist Party to become legal in 1981. However, Islamist groups were specifically banned from participating in elections. Tunisia's first multiparty elections did not bring about much change. The ruling party got 95 percent of the total vote.

Economic problems continued to create trouble for Bourguiba's weakening government. In 1984 the government decided to reduce subsidies (money paid by the government to producers to keep consumer prices low) on basic food items such as bread. As a result, prices rose, and the unemployed and rural poor were particularly hard hit. Riots broke out in southern Tunisia, during which about 90 Tunisians were killed and another 900 injured. The government declared a state of emergency, and Bourguiba had to announce on television that the price of bread would decrease.

Immediately after the riots, Brigadier General Zine El Abidine Ben Ali was appointed director of national security. Ben Ali had a reputation for being very tough on domestic security issues, but there were concerns about giving a military figure so much power. The general aggressively led security forces against Islamist groups, focusing on eliminating their leadership. Trained in the United States, Ben Ali was not only an important military leader but also a political figure. At this time, Tunisia's different branches of government—the army, security forces, and the ruling party—all competed for power, as Tunisia seemed poised for new leadership. Bourguiba's failing health added to the lack of unified control of the government.

BEN ALI TAKES OVER

By 1986 it was clear that serious economic problems and the failing health of Bourguiba had diminished the leadership of the ruling party. At the same time, Ben Ali had gained enough political control to have himself appointed prime minister. In 1987 Ben Ali deposed Bourguiba, on the grounds that the president was senile.

Tunisian president Zine El Abidine Ben Ali at the 2001 Arab League summit in Jordan. Since assuming power in a bloodless coup in 1987, Ben Ali has for the most part followed the leadership path charted by his predecessor, Habib Bourguiba.

The transition of power was peaceful, although concerns arose that Tunisia's long tradition of keeping the military out of politics would change with this switch in leadership.

Even though President Ben Ali brought new leadership, the ruling party remained in power. Though he did change the name of the Destourian Socialist Party to the Constitutional Democratic Rally (RCD), he continued to lead Tunisia along the lines established by Bourguiba. At first, Ben Ali's primary focus as president was economic reform, especially with regard to encouraging foreign investment and diminishing state control. The changes produced enhanced growth.

On the foreign policy front, Ben Ali maintained Tunisia's traditional moderate stance on Arab-Israeli issues. Following the Israeli-Palestinian agreements in 1993–94, Tunisia established low-level diplomatic relations with Israel. These lasted until fall 2000, when, following the outbreak of sustained Palestinian-Israeli violence, Tunisia severed its links.

Under Ben Ali's leadership, relations with neighboring Libya improved. These relations had been especially tense earlier in the decade, following a Libyan attempt to overthrow the Tunisian regime. In 1989 Tunisia joined Algeria, Morocco, Libya, and Mauritania in the Arab Maghreb Union. Relations with nations of the West have remained strong, as investment from Western companies has been important to Tunisia's economic growth.

While Ben Ali's leadership has brought some improvements to the Tunisian economy, the Tunisian regime continues to brook no real opposition. Ben Ali legalized several opposition parties, but he has carefully controlled political life. In 1994 the government arrested political dissidents before scheduled elections and continued to crack down hard on Islamist groups, which had scored successes in the 1989 parliamentary elections. As a result, Ben Ali ran uncontested. In 1999 Ben Ali was reelected, after running against two token candidates from opposition parties; he won nearly 100 percent of the vote. Although he had previously announced he would retire in 2004, he ran for a fourth term that year and was reelected with almost 95 percent of the vote. (The chief opposition, the Democratic Progressive Party, had withdrawn from the election in a boycott.)

Once known throughout the Muslim world for its tolerant, cosmopolitan culture, Tunisia struggles to reconcile its internal divisions. In 2002 a Jewish synagogue in Tunis was destroyed by a bomb, and al-Qaeda, an international Islamist terrorist group, took responsibility. In 2007, 12 Islamist militants, believed to be from Algeria, were killed in a gunfight with Tunis security forces. Notwithstanding Ben Ali's critics, few Tunisians appear to favor the path of violent, revolutionary change.

Tunisia's cultural heritage has created a people who value order and tradition as well as modernization and enterprise. Its history of avoiding bloody civil conflict and of balancing its Islamic heritage with an openness to change from the outside gives it the potential to liberalize its politics and social life while maintaining overall stability. But creation of a truly democratic society remains a formidable challenge.

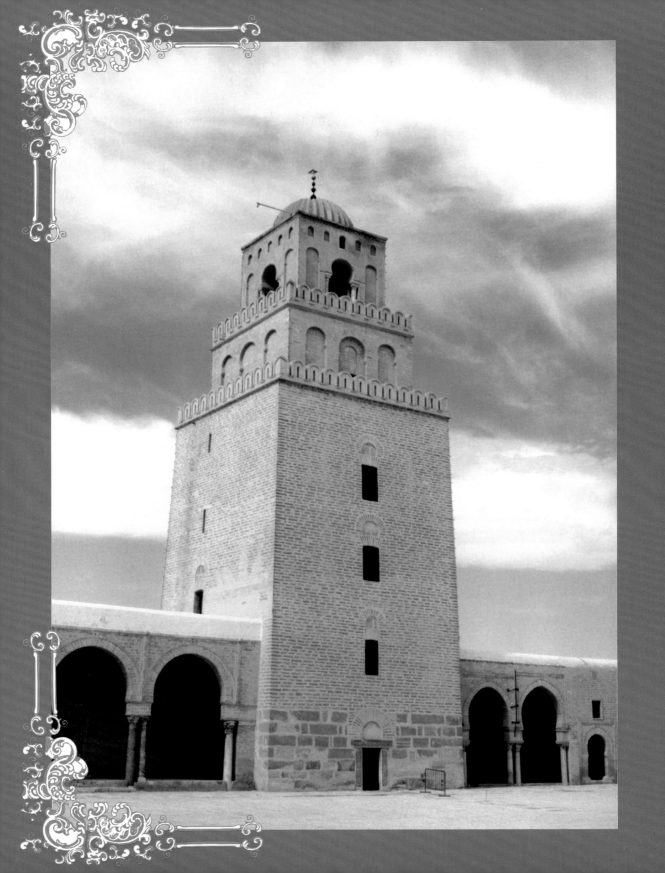

The world's oldest surviving minaret is located in Kairouan, sometimes called the fourth major city in Islam (after Mecca, Medina, and Jerusalem). The mosque was constructed in A.D. 670, and the minaret was built around 730. By that time, the Islamic faith had spread throughout North Africa. Islam remains an important part of Tunisian life today.

The Economy, Politics, and Religion

After nearly 50 years of independence, Tunisia has evolved from a poor country to a middle-income nation with a reasonably bright economic outlook. Its economy, which in the past was based primarily on agriculture, now is varied, with important assets not only in agriculture but also in mining, energy, tourism, and manufacturing. Moreover, in Tunisia problems that have plagued many Arab, African, and developing nations appear to be under control. The percentage of Tunisians living below the government-established poverty line is low (an estimated 7 percent in the year 2005); the economy has been growing at a healthy rate (an annual average of more than 5 percent between 1997 and 2001); and inflation is manageable (an estimated 3.1 percent in 2007). Unemployment, however, remains a chronic problem.

ECONOMIC OVERVIEW

In 2007 the CIA estimated Tunisia's **gross domestic product (GDP)** at $77 billion. GDP, the total value of goods and services produced in a one-year period, is an important measure of the overall size of a nation's economy. In 2007 Tunisia had the world's 74th-largest economy.

Because GDP is linked closely to population (more people generate more economic activity), it has limited use in judging the prosperity of a nation's people. A better statistic for measuring that is GDP per capita, obtained by dividing GDP by population. In 2007 Tunisia's estimated GDP per capita—each citizen's average share of the nation's economic activity—stood at $7,500. This is rather low by U.S. and Western standards (by comparison 2007 GDP per capita in the United States was estimated at $45,800 and in France, Tunisia's former colonial master, at $33,200). But worldwide Tunisia ranks among middle-income countries.

INVESTMENT, PRIVATIZATION, AND TRADE

One key to Tunisia's recent economic success has been its ability to attract foreign investment. Among the factors that appeal to investors—especially from Europe, Japan, and the United States—is Tunisia's modern infrastructure, which ensures that goods can be transported efficiently and inexpensively. Tunisia boasts a good highway system and six major seaports: Tunis-La Goulette, Bizerte, Sfax, Sousse, Skhira, and Gabès. In fact, Tunisia was ranked as the most competitive country in Africa by the World Economic Forum 2000–2001 Report, and again in 2008.

Investors also like Tunisia's climate of political and social stability, as well as recent legislation that offers foreign investors special consideration on taxes and customs. That legislation is part of a long-term development strategy geared toward reducing government control of the economy. During the rule of Habib Bourguiba, the government managed many segments of the Tunisian economy, and one result was inefficiency. Particularly since the early 1990s, the administration of Ben Ali has promoted privatization efforts—shifting ownership of government-controlled industry into the hands of private investors.

Under Ben Ali's leadership, Tunisia has taken steps to increase trade with foreign countries. It signed an association agreement with the European Union (EU) that called for the gradual elimination of trade barriers between Tunisia and the EU, with the ultimate

A donkey pulls a gas tank in Hammamet. Tunisia's first oil field was discovered in 1964 in the southern region of the country, near the border with Algeria. Today, the country is estimated to have oil reserves of 1.7 billion barrels. Shell is one of five international oil companies that distribute fuel and refined petroleum products in Tunisia along with the state-owned oil company, Société Nationale de Distribution du Pétrole (SNDP); the others are Total, Mobil, Elf, and Esso Tunisia.

goal of establishing a free-trade zone. Tunisia also signed agreements to implement free-trade areas with Morocco, Egypt, Jordan, Libya, and Mauritania.

MAJOR ECONOMIC SECTORS

Though not nearly as important now as previously, agriculture continues to play a significant role in Tunisia's economy. It accounts for about 12 percent of the nation's GDP and employs more than half of Tunisia's workers. Olives, olive oil, grain, dairy products, tomatoes, citrus fruit, beef, sugar beets, dates, and almonds are among the country's major agricultural products.

Tunisia is well known for its handicrafts, including woven carpets with intricate designs such as the one pictured here.

Tunisia's once-neglected industrial sector grew rapidly after independence. Today industry contributes about 26 percent of Tunisia's GDP and employs nearly one in four Tunisian workers. Particularly important are the petroleum and natural gas industries. Tunisian oil fields were first developed during the 1960s, and the country benefited from the spike in petroleum prices in the 1970s. Tunisia's natural gas industry developed more recently. Tunisia also has a significant mining industry whose primary minerals include iron ore and phosphates (used in fertilizers). Most of the country's phosphate mines are located in the west-central and southwest regions.

More than 10,000 manufacturing companies operate in Tunisia. Textiles, shoes, and leather are the most important manufactured products, followed by processed food, mechanical and electrical products, building materials, and rubber. New growth sectors, such as electronics, automotive components, and chemicals (especially fertilizers), have quickly developed alongside the more traditional forms of manufacturing.

Tunisia has long been known for handicrafts, including textiles, rugs, pottery, leather goods, jewelry, and embroidery. For the most part, these traditional handicrafts are decorative and are exported or sold in the tourist trade. Different cities continue to specialize in certain crafts; for example, Kairouan is known for its carpets.

Tourism has been a major contributor to Tunisia's economic growth. Major tourist attractions include the beaches of the east coast, Jerba Island, the oases in the Tunisian Sahara Desert, and a variety of ancient Roman ruins and Ottoman-era mosques throughout the country. Europeans in particular have flocked to Tunisia's beautiful beaches and pumped money into the Tunisian economy. But not all Tunisians are happy about this: Islamists have objected to the immodesty of beachgoers as being against the cultural norms of Islam.

CONTINUING ECONOMIC CHALLENGES

Despite its generally healthy state, Tunisia's economy is not without problems. The coastal region continues to be far more developed than inland regions, and people who live inland are as a rule much poorer than those on the coast. After independence, the gap between the rich and the poor grew wider, which is not unusual for societies experiencing rapid economic growth. Resentment against those who made huge fortunes helped fuel the Islamist movement of the 1980s. In spite of the recent expansion of the economy, the gap between rich and poor persists.

Unemployment has also been a chronic problem—estimated in 2007 at more than 14 percent. The inability to find work at home has caused many Tunisians to immigrate to Western Europe and oil-rich Arab states. Their remittances (the money they send home to support their families) help bolster the Tunisian economy.

POLITICS

Although Tunisia is a republic with an ostensibly representative government (all citizens over 20 years old have the right to vote), the ruling party—whether going by the name Neo-Destour Party, Destourian Socialist Party (PSD), or Democratic Constitutional Rally (RCD)—has never faced serious political opposition. The Neo-Destour Party's prominent role in winning Tunisia's independence from France in 1956 lent the ruling party a degree of prestige and legitimacy for many years afterward. Even as support for the party began to weaken in the 1970s, its monopoly on governing remained intact, and by law all other political parties were banned.

The law was changed in 1981, opening up Tunisia's parliament to members of opposition political parties. But opposition candidates still face long odds. In the 1999 election, for example, the ruling party—Zine El Abidine Ben Ali's RCD—won more than 80 percent of

The Economy of Tunisia

Gross domestic product (GDP*): $77 billion

GDP per capita: $7,500

Inflation: 3.1%

Natural resources: petroleum, phosphates, iron ore, lead, zinc, salt

Agriculture (11.67% of GDP): olives, olive oil, grain, dairy products, tomatoes, citrus fruit, beef, sugar beets, dates, and almonds

Industry (25.77% of GDP): petroleum, mining (phosphates and iron ore), tourism, textiles, footwear, food, beverages, agribusiness

Services (62.8% of GDP): government services, banking

Foreign trade:

Imports—$18.03 billion: machinery and equipment, hydrocarbons (oil and natural gas), chemicals, food, textiles

Exports—$15.15 billion: textiles, mechanical goods, phosphates and chemicals, agricultural products, hydrocarbons, clothing, electrical equipment

Currency exchange rate: 1.2603 Tunisian dinars = U.S. $1 (Sept. 2008)

*GDP, or gross domestic product, is the total value of goods and services produced in a country annually. All figures are 2007 estimates unless otherwise noted.
Sources: World Bank; CIA World Factbook 2008; Bloomberg.com.

the seats. The year 1999 also marked the first time opposition candidates were permitted to run against an incumbent president. Ben Ali won in a landslide, receiving almost 100 percent of the vote. This is not necessarily a sign of his popularity among Tunisians but rather an indication of the level of democratic choice available to voters. Restrictions on the freedom of the press limit the opportunities that opposition parties have to put forth their views.

Nevertheless, opposition parties did garner 37 of the 182 seats in the 1999 parliamentary elections. The Movement of Democratic Socialists (MDS) won 13 seats, the Unionist Democratic Union

(UDU) won 7 seats, and all other opposition parties won a total of 14 seats. The Islamist party Al Nahda, which the government alleges has been involved in subversive activities, is outlawed. How much popular support the Islamists enjoy remains unclear, though Al Nahda–affiliated candidates who officially ran as independents won 14 percent of the vote in the 1989 parliamentary elections.

THE STRUCTURE OF GOVERNMENT

The Tunisian government has three branches: executive, legislative, and judicial. The executive branch is led by the president, who is also the chief of state. In general, the president dominates all three branches of the government, with extensive legislative and judicial authority. In the case of a perceived threat to the republic, Tunisia's constitution gives the president broad emergency powers. Presidents are elected by popular vote for a five-year term. The president appoints the prime minister, who leads the government in day-to-day

Tunisia's legislative branch, the 182-seat Chamber of Deputies, meets in this building in Tunis. All citizens over age 20 are permitted to vote for their representatives.

The Tunisian flag was originally adopted in 1835. The white disk in the center contains a crescent moon and a five-pointed star, both of which are Islamic symbols. The color red was a symbol of resistance against Ottoman rule. Tunisia's 1959 constitution made this the flag of the newly independent nation.

affairs. The prime minister is the leader of the president's appointed advisers, the Council of Ministers.

Tunisia's legislative branch is the 182-seat Chamber of Deputies. Its members are elected by popular vote to a five-year term coinciding with that of the president. Frequently, members of the Chamber of Deputies have also been selected to serve in the Council of Ministers, in the executive branch. The Chamber of Deputies elects from its membership four permanent committees covering political affairs, cultural affairs, economic affairs, and general legislation. They study the issues and report back to the full Chamber. The Chamber of Deputies generally does not initiate legislation and usually approves without argument any legislation proposed by the president.

Tunisia's judicial branch has four levels of courts. The highest legal authority is the Court of Cassation, a panel of three judges that considers decisions by lower courts. The executive branch and the president strongly influence the judiciary, particularly in sensitive political cases. The Tunisian legal system is based largely on the French civil law system.

The secular approach to law in Tunisia is criticized by Islamists, who wish to see a return to a stricter observance of **Sharia** (Islamic law). In particular, laws governing the role of women have come under attack by Islamists. The Tunisian Code of Personal Status gave Tunisian women many rights unusual for a Muslim country. Today, women have public roles that Islamists find objectionable. For example, after the 2004 elections, women held 43 out of 189 seats in the Chamber of Deputies, or nearly 23 percent.

HUMAN RIGHTS ISSUES

In the first quarter century after independence, the Tunisian government was a one-party system, and any opposition was treated as a threat to the country's stability. Criminal investigations, arrests, judicial proceedings, and travel controls, including denial of passports, discouraged public criticism of the government. 3The government also deterred newspapers and magazines from publishing material that it considered undesirable. It even seized editions of foreign newspapers containing articles to which it objected.

To a certain extent, those tactics have continued. The government's human rights record has been uneven, and it has committed serious abuses. During the 1994 election campaign, the government arrested many political dissidents, targeting Islamist groups. The Islamists are perceived as the strongest opposition movement to the Tunisian government and the greatest threat to internal security.

The police, called the Surete Nationale, share responsibility for internal security with a paramilitary national guard, which is called the Garde Nationale. The police operate in the capital and a few other cities. In outlying areas, the police work with the Garde Nationale. Both forces are under the control of the minister of the interior and the president. The security forces have been responsible for serious human rights abuses.

Ben Ali's government has made some effort to defuse growing

demands to reform the political system. In 1988, for example, Tunisia's constitution was amended to do away with life presidency and automatic succession. Freedom of expression was guaranteed, and laws were rewritten to give journalists more opportunity to do investigative reporting. Whether the Tunisian government is ready to tolerate the freedoms it claims to value, however, remains to be seen.

THE IMPORTANCE OF ISLAM

While Tunisia has a secular government that has muzzled Islamist opposition, the country is unquestionably part of the Islamic culture that dominates the Middle East and North Africa. About 98 percent of Tunisians are Muslims; about 1 percent are

The Five Pillars of Islam

Shahada—the statement that there is only one God and Muhammad was his last prophet. Islam recognizes prophets from the biblical tradition, including Abraham (Ibrahim), Moses (Musa), and Jesus (Isa).

Salat—the prayer performed five times a day in a special posture—at sunrise, midday, afternoon, sunset, and evening. The faithful must bow and face Mecca. The *muezzin* gives the call to prayer at appropriate times.

Zakat—donations to charity. Muslims are charged with giving 2.5 percent of their income above basic necessities to build and maintain mosques and help the poor. Religious foundations called *waqfs* administer contributions of property.

Sawm—daytime fasting during the month of Ramadan. In Tunisia, fasting is a matter of personal conscience, not a state-enforced law.

Hajj—the pilgrimage to Mecca. Muslims, if they are able, are supposed to do this once in their lifetime, during the 12th month of the lunar calendar.

Christian and 1 percent are Jewish. In spite of the recent wave of Islamist activity in Tunisia, Christian and Jewish communities have traditionally practiced their faith freely and contributed to Tunisia's rich cultural diversity.

In the past, Tunisia was an important center for Islamic learning. The Zitouna Mosque in Tunis was a focal point for Islamic studies, and more than 20,000 Islamic schools, or *madrasas*, operated throughout Tunisia. Although many experts on the country say that cosmopolitan Tunisian society was never drawn to a strict interpretation of Islam, in recent years there has been a push for a more rigorous practice of Islam, especially among younger people.

In Islam, the community of believers is called the **umma**. Today, this community is very large and reaches from the Middle East to North Africa, Southeast Asia, North America, and Europe. There

A Tunisian girl teaches her younger sister to read the Qur'an. Nearly all of the inhabitants of the country are Muslims.

are two major branches of Islam, Sunni and Shia, with significant differences in belief about how the *umma* should be led. The vast majority of Tunisia's Muslims belong to the Sunni branch, which also claims the most believers worldwide.

Whether Sunni or Shia, however, Muslims share a belief in the importance of the Five Pillars of Islam, fundamental obligations of prayer and faith.

For Muslims, ethical conduct includes behavior that is generous, fair, honest, and respectful, especially in terms of family relations. Islam forbids adultery, gambling, usury, and the consuming of pork or alcohol. The Qur'an, or Koran (the holy book of Islam), the **Hadith** (the sayings and teachings of Muhammad), and the *sunna* (the example of Muhammad's personal behavior) form a guide to spiritual, ethical, and social behavior for Sunni Muslims.

The mosque is a building for worship, as well as a place of meeting and study. Often attached to a mosque is a *madrasa*, a Muslim school for the study of Islamic scripture. Kairouan, the first Arab center in the Maghreb, had a great mosque built on the classical design, with an open courtyard leading to a covered space. Attached to the building is a minaret, from which the muezzin called the faithful to prayer five times a day.

Even in a relatively secular nation like Tunisia, the call to prayer is broadcast on radio and television, interrupting programming. Friday is the holy day of communal prayer. People often do not go to work but rather to the mosque for prayer sessions. Any adult male who knows the prayer forms can lead prayers. A man who regularly leads prayers is called an *imam*.

Sharia, the Arabic word for "correct path," has come to mean the religious law. Beginning in the 1980s, countries throughout the Middle East and the Maghreb experienced a strong Islamic revival, with many devout Muslims wanting the laws of their country to follow *Sharia*. In Tunisia this movement may not have succeeded in transforming government or society, but it has had a significant impact on the political situation. Tunisian Islamist groups such as the outlawed Al Nahda, which means Renaissance, believe that social problems like poverty are the result of secularism. They advocate a return to the simple Muslim values of cooperation, hard work, and piety. They believe that economic and social development in Tunisia must take into account religious values, and they see the Tunisian Code of Personal Status as a corruption, not a reform, of Islamic law. However, most Tunisian Islamists appear to believe that their goals can be accomplished through education rather than violence.

The Tunisian Code of Personal Status

Adopted in 1956, the Code of Personal Status attempted to establish the equality of women and men with respect to marriage and family law by, among other things,

- abolishing polygamy
- granting both spouses the right to request divorce through legal proceedings
- establishing 17 as the minimum age for girls to marry, and providing that they must consent to the marriage
- granting mothers custody of their minor children in the event that the children's father died.

Revisions adopted in the 1990s further strengthened women's rights within the Tunisian family.

OTHER RELIGIONS

Outside of its Sunni Muslim majority, Tunisia has small communities of other religions. For the most part, members of these religious minorities and Muslims have peacefully coexisted for many years. The 1 percent of Tunisians who practice the Christian faith are largely Roman Catholics of French ethnicity. Tunisia's once-thriving community of Jews has largely disappeared as the result of emigration after the first Arab-Israeli war in the late 1940s. The Jews of the island of Jerba, who live according to age-old traditions, are one of the last remnants of the Jewish communities once scattered throughout the Maghreb. Unfortunately, violence from the Arab-Israeli conflict has spilled over into Tunisia, and Jewish synagogues have been the targets of anti-Israeli passions.

A Tunisian family relaxes at home; the women drink tea while young boys play a game of Monopoly.

The People

odern Tunisia is fairly homogenous—that is, most people share similar values and beliefs and come from a similar background. At the same time, Tunisians are a blend of many cultures. The Berbers were the original inhabitants of Tunisia, but the immigration of Phoenicians, Jews, Romans, Vandals, and Arabs over the centuries created a unique Tunisian cultural identity. Today, only a few Berber villages remain in Tunisia, on the island of Jerba and in a few communities at the edge of the Sahara. Modern Tunisian people think of themselves as Arabs, but they are proud of the Berber, African, and European influences that are part of their heritage.

LANGUAGES

The official language of Tunisia is Arabic, but there are many varieties or dialects of the language in use around the country. Classical Arabic is the language of the Qur'an. A simplified version of Classical Arabic, called Modern Literary Arabic, serves as the language of government, the media, and most education. In their daily lives, most Tunisians speak a form of Arabic called "intermediary," a mixture of Modern Literary Arabic and a Tunisian dialect of Arabic.

Because of Tunisia's former colonial ties to France, knowledge of the French language is widespread. French used to be the language of higher education and urban society, but the recent Islamic revival has done much to restore the importance of the Arabic language in those spheres. French continues to be used in commerce.

Increased tourism and foreign investment in Tunisia have made English a more common third language among a growing number of Tunisians, and many also speak Italian. Today, Berber-speaking people make up less than 1 percent of the population, and the Berber language, Chelha, is heard only in remote villages.

THE INTERIOR AND THE COAST

Traditionally, Tunisian society was divided between the interior and the coast. This corresponded with the more ancient division between the nomadic peoples of the interior

The People of Tunisia

Population: 10,383,577
Ethnic groups: Arab, 98%; European, 1%; Jewish and other, 1%
Age structure:
    0–14 years: 23.2%
    15–64 years: 69.7%
    65 years and over: 7.1%
Population growth rate: 0.989%
Birth rate: 15.5 births/1,000 population
Death rate: 5.17 deaths/1,000 population
Infant mortality rate: 23.43 deaths/1,000 live births
Life expectancy at birth:
    total population: 75.56 years
    males: 73.79 years
    females: 77.46 years
Total fertility rate: 1.73 children born per woman
Literacy: (age 15 and older who can read and write): 74.3% (2004 est.)

All figures are 2008 estimates unless otherwise indicated.
Source: CIA World Factbook, 2008.

and the settled residents of the coastal towns and cities.

Until recently, tremendous differences in attitude and outlook persisted between people who lived in the rural, undeveloped regions of Tunisia's interior and those who lived along Tunisia's lengthy coastline. Those who lived along the coast tended to be better educated, wealthier, and more outward oriented, and those who lived in the interior of Tunisia were poorer and more traditional.

The people of the coast lived in trading communities or prosperous farming villages. Over the centuries, the port cities had more contact with the Mediterranean world through trade, exchanging skills, knowledge, and customs that made them relatively cosmopolitan. A merchant class developed in these communities, comparable to that found in European towns. Skilled craftsmen shared

The Berbers who lived in southeastern Tunisia built their homes next to—and in some cases, into—the sides of mountains.

knowledge of their trades in guilds, just as Europeans did during the Middle Ages. The farms of the Northern Tell and the coastal plains were productive, and farmers often owned their own land and were able to live above the subsistence level. Inland, the lives of pastoral herders and small farmers changed very little over the centuries.

In recent decades economic growth has fueled a steady rise in the standard of living of Tunisia's citizens, especially in urban areas. Unlike many other North African countries, Tunisian society has a large middle class. Economic growth has not affected rural lives as much. The government has worked to bring modern life to Tunisian rural communities in the interior, but large numbers of people have migrated to the coastal cities in search of a better standard of living. While many have been successful, others crowd into the shantytowns called **gourbivilles** on the outskirts of most Tunisian cities. Like their rural relations, these people are more oriented toward traditional Islam and the Arab world.

DIVISIONS

Tunisian society can be divided into four main socioeconomic groupings. These four groups have their roots in the divisions that have existed in Tunisian culture for centuries. At the top are members of the old notable families, who frequently can trace their ancestry back to the original Arab conquerors of Tunisia. Second are the members of the upper middle class, which is made up of Western-educated professionals and politicians, prominent businesspeople, and large landowners. The third group, the middle

(Opposite) Most of Tunisia's population is clustered around the fertile area along the Mediterranean coast, as this map illustrates. Because it is a small country geographically, Tunisia is much more densely populated than its neighbors Algeria and Libya.

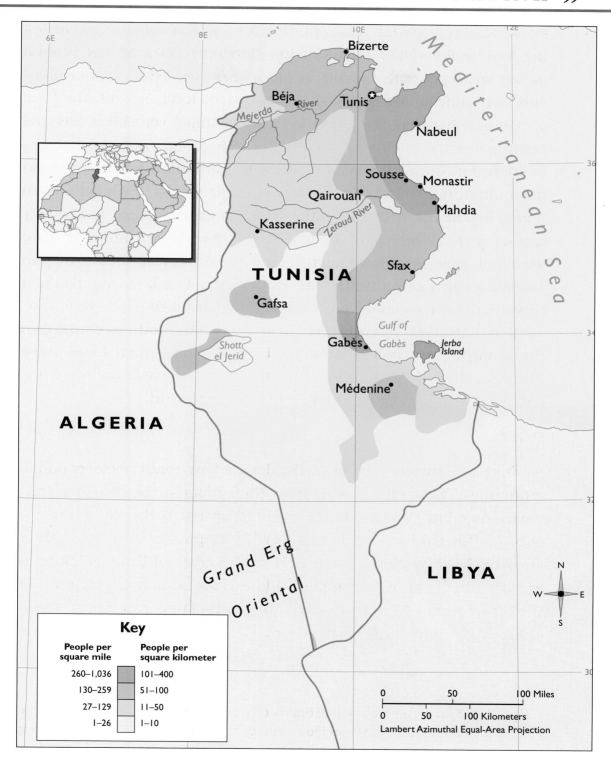

Bizerte

Béja   River   Tunis

Mejerda

Nabeul

Sousse   Monastir

Qairouan   Mahdia

Kasserine   Zeroud River

TUNISIA

Gafsa

Sfax

Gulf of

Gabès   Gabès   Jerba
Island

Shott
el Jerid

Médenine

ALGERIA

Grand Erg

Oriental   LIBYA

N
W   E
S

Mediterranean Sea

Key

People per
square mile

People per
square kilometer

260–1,036	101–400
130–259	51–100
27–129	11–50
1–26	1–10

0   50   100 Miles

0   50   100 Kilometers

Lambert Azimuthal Equal-Area Projection

6E   8E   10E   12E

36

34

32

30

class, is composed of teachers, small-business owners and shop-keepers, independent farmers, and skilled workers. At the bottom of the socioeconomic ladder are agricultural workers, subsistence farmers, and the unemployed.

Today, Tunisian society has also become somewhat divided along generational lines. Because of a high birthrate after independence in 1956, Tunisia had a large population of young people beginning their working careers during the 1980s, a period of economic downturn. Although many of these young people were better educated than their parents, they found few opportunities for professional careers. Discontented with their prospects in Tunisian society, many immigrated to Europe. For those who stayed, Islamist movements offered hope for changing their society.

This situation has started to improve, as birthrates dropped beginning in the 1970s. At the same time, education levels have

A selection of colorful goods woven in Tunisia.

continued to improve. Expectations among young people for finding good jobs are high. Nonetheless, there are more Tunisians qualified for professional positions than there are such positions, one reason young Tunisians continue to leave their country.

MEN, WOMEN, AND THE FAMILY

In spite of generational differences, the family remains the basic unit of Tunisian society. The social life and sense of identity of most Tunisians centers on their family. In the past, the extended family—which might include in the same household grandparents, parents, children, and other close relatives—was the norm. Recent changes in attitudes—including greater individualism among educated young people, a desire among women for more freedom, and an increased emphasis on romantic love in marriage—have challenged the traditional role of the family in Tunisia. Today, the nuclear family (consisting only of a father, mother, and their children) is becoming more important in Tunisia. However, family traditions remain strong, and extended families still provide tremendous economic and emotional support.

In Muslim society, marriage is the foundation for family life. Traditionally, having children gave women status and security, so beginning married life as soon as possible was important. Marriages were arranged by the fathers of the bride and groom, as marriage was seen as a family choice, not a personal decision for the two young people getting married. Today, arranged marriages are still common among rural families. By contrast, urban people increasingly expect to choose their own marriage partners, although they might consult with their families before marrying. Once married, they tend to live in nuclear rather than extended families. This trend, combined with rising educational levels and economic development, helped to lower birthrates in Tunisia and improved the status of women. Because of the Code of Personal

Status, women can be the legal head of a household in Tunisia, which is very unusual in an Islamic country.

The Code of Personal Status changed the structure of traditional Muslim family relations when it became part of Tunisia's constitution. In traditional Muslim society, a man can have as many as four wives. A husband has a great deal of legal control over his wife, and he can divorce a wife simply by saying, "I repudiate thee." Custody of children after a divorce usually goes to the husband. These customs are not so much part of Islamic religious law as they are part of the tribal culture of the Arabian Peninsula that made men the head of the family and the tribe. The Berber tribal culture of ancient Tunisia was very different. Women were able to be the head of the family and even the tribe.

Possibly, this ancient heritage contributed toward changing the role of women in Tunisian society. The Code of Personal Status states that men and women are equal before the law. It reformed many Islamic family customs—for example, by abolishing polygamy, granting both spouses the right to request divorce, setting the minimum age for marriage at 17 for girls, and providing that they must consent to the marriage. Because of this law, Tunisian women are more independent and are more able to pursue their own careers than are most women in Islamic countries. New amendments announced in 1992 have strengthened the place of women still further, eliminating legal provisions that could be interpreted as unfair and sexist. This law has less of an effect on rural women, whose lives tend to be more traditional.

Islamic culture makes a clear distinction between the public world of men and the domestic world of women. Gender separation is part of a traditional Muslim life. Today, many Tunisian men and women interact in public at universities, in the workplace, on public transportation, and at some social events. Compared with their counterparts in other Arab societies, Tunisian women are more integrated into the public world of work, and some pursue careers as lawyers, doctors, teachers, and businesswomen.

However, the majority of Tunisian women still do not have careers outside of the home. Many are better educated than their ancestors, but they spend their adult lives in traditional women's tasks and devote themselves to caring for their families. In spite of the comparatively liberal laws in Tunisia, conservative beliefs about the proper role of women in Islamic society are deeply held. The recent revival of Islam has also encouraged young women to conform to the older Muslim customs.

The social life of most Tunisians revolves around the family, and eating meals together is very important. Lunch is the biggest meal of the day and the preferred time for visiting with friends and family. Men often go to restaurants and coffeehouses with friends.

FOOD AND COOKING

Tunisian cooking, which is characteristically spicy, blends European, Berber, and Middle Eastern culinary traditions. The national dish of Tunisia is couscous, a type of tiny pasta, usually made from semolina. It is cooked in a special kind of double boiler called a *couscousiere*. Meat and vegetables are boiled in the lower half; holes in the top half allow steam to rise and cook the grain. After it is cooked, the grain is piled in the middle of a dish, and the meat and vegetables are served on top.

Many of the cooking styles and utensils in Tunisia developed among nomadic tribes. Their wandering lifestyle meant that they could prepare food only with what few pots and pans they could carry with them. Sometimes, they would make a pot from the earth where they set up camp. One such pot is the conical-lidded *tagine*. Today, *tagine* also refers to the casserole-type dish cooked in this kind of pot.

During his 1914 visit to Tunisia, the Swiss Expressionist artist Paul Klee (1879–1940) painted this watercolor picture, *St. Germain at Tunis.*

CHILDREN AND EDUCATION

While most men go to work and most women work at home, most Tunisian children attend school. Education in Tunisia is free and accessible to everyone. By law, schooling is required for children between the ages of 6 and 16. Primary school classes are conducted in Arabic. After primary school, most classes are taught in Arabic and French.

In Tunisia, education has been a priority in the national budget since independence. By the early 21st century three-fourths of Tunisians age 15 and older could read and write. Recent reforms of the educational system have led to more schools in rural areas, a greater percentage of girls in school, and a curriculum with more emphasis on the sciences and vocational training. The government sees education as the best way to prepare Tunisia for the future.

THE ARTS

From literature to painting to music, the arts in Tunisia have been greatly influenced by the country's mix of cultures. Tunisian museums are filled with examples of art from the Roman and

Ottoman eras, as well as modern art that frequently synthesizes the many influences of Tunisia's past.

Literature is important to Tunisian culture because the power of the written word is crucial to the Islamic faith. Arabic writers have been producing great poetry for more than 1,000 years. An often-quoted *hadith* from the prophet Muhammad says that the ink of the

Fans of the popular Star Wars films might recognize these buildings in the Tunisian desert; they were part of the movie set. Director George Lucas filmed a large part of the first episode, *A New Hope*, in Tunisia. "When I was searching in 1977 for a place to make the first Star Wars movie," Lucas later recalled, "I found Tunisia the ideal country for filming: beautiful countryside, unique architecture and a very high level of technical sophistication." Lucas returned to film scenes for *The Phantom Menace* (1999) and *Attack of the Clones* (2002). Over the years Tunisia has been used as a location for many other films, including *The English Patient, Raiders of the Lost Ark, The Life of Brian, and Jesus of Nazareth.*

writer is more precious than the blood of the warrior. Today, most contemporary Tunisian authors write in French, even when their subject is the heritage of colonialism. Arabic is reserved for religious subjects.

Architectural styles show the tremendous range of cultural influences in Tunisia. Scattered throughout the country are **Punic** and Roman ruins, whose orderly shapes influence the architecture of modern urban buildings. The Moorish elegance of Islamic architecture is found in the Arab **medinas**, the older parts of most Tunisian cities. Even the original inhabitants of Tunisia contributed to its architectural wealth. In the south, the Berber structures carved into sandstone cliffs are of great interest to tourists.

For many years, the French colonial presence dominated Tunisian culture. Under the French, many Europeans went to Tunisia to paint. Perhaps the most famous was Paul Klee, who first visited in 1914. In 1935 a group of Tunisian painters who had studied in Paris returned to Tunisia to found the Tunisian school. Rather than mimicking European styles, their canvases followed Tunisian folklore patterns found in traditional textiles. Today, painting is a well-established contemporary art medium in Tunisia. This is somewhat unusual in a Muslim country because Islam prohibits the representation of the human form in art.

In addition to painting, a broader revival of traditional Tunisian culture began in the 1930s. Because traditional handicrafts began dying out at the beginning of the 20th century, the government intervened to support these traditional art forms. Today, traditional handicrafts mostly target the tourist trade. Leatherwork, brass and copper fixtures, and woven textiles, especially rugs, are all part of the traditional arts in Tunisia.

For a long time, Tunisia lacked a strong dramatic tradition. Conservative Muslim leaders disapproved of the traditional puppet shadow theater, so it was not part of the cultural revival of the

1930s. However, theater has become part of contemporary Tunisian culture. In the 1960s urban youth began to develop dramatic troupes, drawing audiences from radio and television. In addition, Tunisians have begun to create their own movie industry. Several popular American movies, including the Academy Award–winning *The English Patient* and parts of the Star Wars series, have been filmed in Tunisia. And since 1962 Tunisia has sponsored its own film festival, the Carthage Film Festival.

Tunisia's diverse musical traditions reflect a wide variety of cultures. *Nouba* came from the Andalusian culture that developed in medieval Spain and was brought to Tunisia by immigrants in the 16th century. *Malouf* (meaning "normal" in Arabic) is an Arab style of traditional music that is popular in Tunisia. *Bachraf*, which is of Turkish origin, became part of Tunisian culture during the Ottoman period. Contemporary Tunisian musicians have been influenced by American jazz.

The vibrancy of the arts in Tunisia demonstrates the cosmopolitan nature of Tunisian culture.

A mosque on a green square in Sfax, Tunisia's second-largest city. Sfax is an important industrial center and one of the country's major ports.

Communities

Tunisia's farms and olive groves once fed the empires of the Mediterranean world. Today, relatively few Tunisians continue to live in farming communities: more than two-thirds of the country's roughly 10 million people reside in urban areas. That is not to suggest that Tunisia's cities sprang up recently, however. For several millennia, ships have been coming into Tunisian ports to exchange their goods. Most of Tunisia's modern cities are located along the country's lengthy coastline, many on the sites of the ancient cities.

Phoenician traders established some of the Tunisian cities we know today up to 3,000 years ago. Other cities were established by waves of conquerors—the Romans, Byzantines, Arabs, Ottomans, and French—who all controlled Tunisia at one time in its history. As the power of each of these distinct cultures rose and fell, the cities of Tunisia evolved, absorbing the architectural styles and urban order of the conquerors.

During the Ottoman period, Tunisian cities took on several distinguishing characteristics. The cities were divided into quarters, with people who shared a common bond, such as religion or ethnicity, tending to live in the same quarter. Houses were often made of brick or mud brick, and walls, doors, and ceilings were decorated. Often the wood of shutters, doors, and window sashes was painted a characteristic blue. These features can still be found in the medina, or old section, of many of Tunisia's cities.

A row of *ghorfas* in Metameur, a town in southern Tunisia. The Berbers built *ghorfas* as fortified storage places for grain and olive oil; these were constructed more than 600 years ago.

TUNIS

With a population of about one million, Tunis is the country's capital and largest city. It is also one of the most cosmopolitan urban centers in the Mediterranean region. About 6 miles (10 km) inland from the Gulf of Tunis, Tunis sits on the shores of a lake that joins it to the Mediterranean Sea. Today, the metropolis is marked by a remarkable mixture of European

> **Tombs of Muslim saints were often centers of religious devotion in North Africa. In Tunis, one of the most important of these shrines was that of Sidi Mahraz, the patron saint of sailors. A great mosque was built over the shrine during Ottoman times.**

and North African cultures. The contrast between the ancient medina and the modern city highlights the long history and contemporary importance of Tunis to the country.

Tunis is an ancient city. Its history goes back to Punic times, when it was second only to Carthage in size and power in the region. After Rome destroyed Carthage, Tunis flourished as part of the Roman Empire. When the Banu Hilal tribe destroyed Kairouan, the capital city of the North African province of the Arab Empire, Tunis became the most important city in the region. It became the capital of the Hafsid dynasty in the 13th century.

Although Tunis was not always Tunisia's political capital, it was a very important religious center from the earliest years of the Arab Empire in the Maghreb. The Ez-Zitouna Mosque, the largest mosque in Tunis, was started by the Umayyad rulers in 732 and finished by the Aghlabids in 864. From the beginning, the Zitouna Mosque was an important Arab center of Islamic learning. Even in Ottoman times, seekers of knowledge came to the Zitouna Mosque. Today, the ancient school of Islamic study associated with the

Zitouna Mosque is now part of the University of Tunis. The mosque remains at the heart of the medina. The souks, or markets, and old city buildings expanded and developed around it.

Much of the shape of the old city of Tunis was formed during the Ottoman period. In the 16th century, Tunis became the center of the Barbary Coast, a base for piracy against European ships in the Mediterranean. Not only the Ottoman sultan but also the bey of Tunis profited from this activity. Some of this wealth helped to build the city we see today.

In modern Tunis, about one-third of the population lives in the medina. This well-preserved section of the city, with its maze of narrow, winding streets and multitude of monuments and historical buildings, has been designated a world heritage site by the United Nations Educational, Scientific and Cultural Organization (UNESCO).

Another third of the population lives in the *ville nouvelle*, the new city, which was built mostly by the French. The new city fans out from Avenue Habib Bourguiba, named for Tunisia's first president; the center of Tunisia's modern government is located there. In the new city, architectural styles range from 19th-century baroque to the futuristic designs of modern architects.

Finally, the poorest third of Tunis's population lives in the shantytowns, or *gourbivilles*, that surround the outskirts of the city. These shantytowns are a feature of many cities in North Africa. The inhabitants live in makeshift houses, often without an adequate supply of water. While many migrant workers expect their lives in the *gourbivilles* to be a temporary stop on the way to a middle-class lifestyle, some families have lived in the shantytowns for generations. The government has worked to improve conditions in this area, especially by providing education and health care for its residents.

In the last 50 years, many rural people have moved to Tunis, and the city has grown considerably. Today, the metropolitan area of Tunis reaches far beyond the official limits of the city, as its suburbs absorb the communities that once surrounded it. La Goulette, a city in its own right, is part of this urban sprawl and serves as Tunis's port. Tunisia's eighth-largest city, L'Ariana, is just north of Tunis and is rapidly becoming absorbed by Tunis's metropolitan area.

Not only have Tunis's area and population grown, but its impor-

The kasbah, or fort, looks down over the town of Le Kef. The main part of the fort was built in the early 17th century, and it was expanded in 1813.

Tunisians enjoy themselves on the beach at Sousse.

tance as an economic center in Tunisia has also expanded. Over a third of the country's manufacturing companies are located in Tunis (the remaining manufacturing operations are spread between the coastal areas and the northwestern and southern regions). Most industry, with the exception of the handicraft industry, is located outside of the city proper.

SFAX

Located on the coast of central Tunisia in the region known as the Sahel, Sfax is the second-largest city in Tunisia, with a population of approximately 270,000. Unlike Tunis, it is not a popular tourist destination. Rather, it is a highly industrialized urban center with an important port for commerce and fishing. Sfax is one of the country's major seaports, handling the export of olive oil and phosphates.

Sfax was originally settled by Phoenician merchants, who traded with the Berber peoples of the interior. Like many cities in Tunisia, Sfax has two distinct sections: the new town and the medina. During Ottoman times, the city grew in importance, and the medina was built up over the old port. The well-preserved medina is one of the most historically authentic in Tunisia. Its souk caters primarily to local people, who still do most of their shopping there.

SOUSSE

Sousse is located on the coast in central Tunisia. With a population of about 173,000, it is Tunisia's third-largest city and an important tourist destination. Its wide beaches and pleasant climate have earned it the nickname "the Pearl of the Sahel." Once a Phoenician trading center, Sousse was shaped by Roman, Byzantine, Arab, and French influences. Like many North African cities, Sousse has a medina and a modern section, built by the French.

The medina is built up around one of the oldest mosques in the Maghreb, called the Ribat. Constructed by Aghlabid rulers in the ninth century, it served as a fortified mosque, defending the port against Sicilian Christian raiders from the north. The Ribat is a rectangular structure, built around a courtyard. Three walls contain small rooms where soldiers once lived; the fourth wall contains the prayer hall. A *nador*, or watchtower, once gave sentries a view of the harbor.

Most museums and points of interest to tourists are located in the medina. Many of the tiny shops in the souk cater to the tourist trade and sell textiles, copper wares, and carpets. The modern section of Sousse, with its mixture of French colonial and modern architecture, has many hotels, as does the strip along the coastline.

The beach near the center of Sousse is popular with local Tunisian families as well as tourists.

BIZERTE

The northernmost city in all of Africa, Bizerte (also known as Bizerta) is the seventh-largest city in Tunisia, with a population of about 114,000 residents. An important port, Bizerte is located on the coast of Cap Blanc, in northern Tunisia. The region between Bizerte and the border of Algeria is known for its rich farmland. Two thousand years ago it was the main supplier of grain to the Roman Empire. The ruins of many ancient Roman towns dot this region.

Founded as a Phoenician trading post, Bizerte was the site of the ancient city of Hyppo-Diarrhytus. The narrow, twisting streets that lead to the old port have not changed much in nearly 1,000 years. The medina, built up during Ottoman times, still contains beautiful mosques, souks, and Moorish houses. The new city, built by the French, has a very different character, with wide avenues, modern buildings, and gardens. Today, Bizerte is one of Tunisia's busiest seaports, handling mostly imports.

KAIROUAN

Kairouan is one of Tunisia's most historic cities. The nation's fifth-largest city, with a population of about 117,000, it is one of the only older cities in Tunisia that is not located on the coast. Thirteen centuries ago, the conquering Arabs established Kairouan, the first Islamic city in the Maghreb, as an outpost in the interior of the region. It was the point of departure for Arab warriors who conquered the Maghreb. From Kairouan, they spread the teachings of Islam and the culture of the Arabian Peninsula among the Berber peoples. Kairouan was the center of a vibrant and sophisticated civilization until the 11th century, when it was nearly destroyed as the Banu Hilal tribe overran the interior of Tunisia.

However, Kairouan's importance as a spiritual center for Muslims has persisted over the centuries. Unlike other Tunisian cities, it has escaped the extremely rapid growth that created many shantytowns. Kairouan is an important manufacturing center and is known for its production of traditional crafts, including rugs, copperware, and shoes. Cobblers in Kairouan are especially famous for making a shoe called the *balgha*, a traditional, flat-soled pointed slipper.

JERBA

Although it is not a city, the island of Jerba is a unique community in Tunisia. One of the few islands off the North African coast, it is situated in the southern part of the country. Jerba has no major cities, although there are several large towns. Most islanders live in villages of whitewashed houses with distinctive conical roofs. Many islanders are of Berber, rather than Arab, stock. They speak the original language of Jerba (also called Jerba), which is a Berber dialect, as well as Arabic. Today, tourism is the major industry on Jerba. Limited water supplies have restricted farming. Traditionally, Jerbans were fishermen and made fine handicrafts.

Unlike the mainland, Jerba has great religious diversity. The island is home to several Christian communities as well as one of the oldest Jewish communities in North Africa. The town of Hara Kbira has about 1,000 Jewish residents, many of whom can trace their ancestry back to the Jews from the Andalusian region of Spain who came to Jerba more than 1,000 years ago. The Jewish synagogue in the village of Hara Sghira has an eighth-century Torah in its possession. In addition to the Jews and Christians, Jerba is home to Kharijite Muslims. The Kharijites were one of the first sects to break away from the main body of Islam, in the eighth century.

CELEBRATIONS

Most celebrations and holidays in Tunisia are connected to the practice of Islam. Some festivals also combine religion with secular observances, such as the coming of spring, the summer harvest, or the fishing season. Festivals are also held on local saints' days, at the tomb of the saint; these celebrations attract Muslims from the surrounding countryside. For example, Mawlid el-Nabi celebrates the birth of the prophet Muhammad. For this festival, families prepare a special pudding of sweetened sorghum to share with friends and family.

Traditional weddings are also important celebrations, emphasizing the importance of family in the Arab world. These wedding festivities can last three to seven days. They include many rituals, including the dying of the bride's hands and feet with henna, a brownish dye, by the women of her family. Afterward, there are visits between the bride's and groom's family, feasting, music, and dancing.

The most important festivals take place during the time of Ramadan. The Islamic year is based on a lunar calendar, so Ramadan falls during different seasons of the year. In the month of Ramadan, Muslims who are no longer children and are in good health practice *sawm*; from dawn until after dark, the devout eat and drink nothing.

At night, the Ramadan celebrations begin. All sorts of delicacies and favorite dishes are served during Ramadan, especially sweets. In Tunisia, a special Ramadan dish is a sweet custard pudding made from sorghum and served with nuts. In the evenings during Ramadan, many families visit with each other and prepare special meals. Wealthier families often entertain large gatherings, using the occasion to display the latest fashions or jewelry.

At the end of Ramadan, one of the most important and joyous

A souk, or market, in the medina of Tunis, the medieval Arab city at the heart of the modern capital of Tunisia. With its narrow, winding streets lined with souks, mosques, schools, cafés, and places of business, the medina of Tunis has been declared a world heritage site by the United Nations Educational, Scientific and Cultural Organization (UNESCO).

Muslim holidays begins. Called Eid al-Fitr, which means "Feast of the Breaking of the Fast," it is a three- or four-day celebration of intense socializing and feasting. Children are given new clothes, and people stay up late into the night visiting with family and friends. Gift-giving and displays of generosity are common. Tunisians are known for their hospitality, and celebrations are an important time for demonstrating this characteristic of Tunisian culture.

French prime minister Jacques Chirac talks with President Bourguiba during a visit to Carthage in 1986. Since Tunisia gained its independence, it has tried to maintain close ties to France and the West, although at times that connection has been strained.

Foreign Relations

Foreign policy in Tunisia has required that this small country balance the demands of three separate and sometimes conflicting areas of concentration: North Africa, the Middle East, and the nations of the West. Being a moderate pro-Western government wedged between the radical anti-Western governments of Algeria and Libya has created security issues for Tunisia. The long-running Arab-Israeli conflict has also affected Tunisia's foreign policy, as Tunisia has sought to both shape and be part of a broad Arab consensus on the issue. Finally, Tunisia's dependence on foreign aid has shaped much of its foreign policy with both wealthier Arab nations and the West—in particular, France and the United States.

Throughout its history as an independent nation, Tunisia has maintained one of the smallest military forces in the Arab world. It has a long history as a peaceful nation, and the warrior tradition of the nomadic Arab tribes was not a large part of Tunisian culture. Today military service is considered a relatively low-status job.

The Tunisian government has never relied on being able to fully defend itself militarily but instead focuses on active diplomacy. Preferring to spend money on domestic programs (more than 60 percent of the budget is devoted to social and development goals), Tunisia has supported a modest military, much more limited in size and combat-effectiveness than those of its neighbors. Tunisia's military includes an army, air force, navy, and national guard. Since the 1980s, the defense policy was oriented toward modernizing its forces, for which it was dependent on aid from the West.

Tunisia's moderate, non-aligned foreign policy is oriented toward promoting economic health rather than supporting any particular political ideology. Tunisia's priorities include working for economic and cultural integration in the Maghreb, promoting agreement and cooperation among Arab nations, and coordinating development with European countries in the Mediterranean region.

Tunisia's primary concern is its relationship with its neighbors in North Africa. Its constitution emphasizes that Tunisia "is part of the Great Arab Maghreb and shall work for its unity within the framework of common interests." The countries of the Maghreb include Tunisia, Algeria, and Morocco as the inner core, plus Libya and Mauritania. They share many cultural similarities as well as economic aspirations. However, the political situation in these countries varies widely. As a result, relations with Algeria and Libya, Tunisia's stronger, larger neighbors, have alternated between periods of tension and harmony.

UNEASY RELATIONS WITH LIBYA

Libya, in particular, has been a cause of concern for Tunisia since the overthrow of the Libyan monarchy in 1969. Tunisia has

Tunisian president Zine El Abidine Ben Ali sits in the Moroccan parliamentary chamber in Rabat before delivering a speech, 1999. Tunisia's relations with Morocco, also a moderate Arab state, have generally been good. Historically, however, there have been tensions between Tunisia and its Maghreb neighbors Libya and Algeria.

alternately sought protection from Libya through alignments with other powers and occasionally attempted to cooperate with Libya's unpredictable leader, Muammar al-Qaddafi. Since he seized power in Libya, Qaddafi has alienated many neighboring states. In 1974 Tunisia rejected his offer to create a political union between the two nations, but Qaddafi did not abandon his hope of controlling his smaller neighbor.

During the 1970s and 1980s, Qaddafi repeatedly attempted to exacerbate Tunisia's internal political tensions. In the 1980s, as many as 2,000 dissident Tunisians bent on overthrowing the Tunisian government trained in Libyan military camps. In 1980 Tunisian dissidents attacked the town of Gafsa, in west-central

Tunisia—a strike planned and supplied by the Libyan government. Tunisia brought a complaint against Libya to the Arab League and the Organization of African Unity, which sought to defuse the crisis between the two countries. However, Libya made no real amends.

Because of chronic unemployment in their home country, many Tunisians worked in the Libyan petroleum industry. Their earnings, sent to families in Tunisia as remittances, were important to Tunisia's economic health. In 1985 Libya's sudden deportation of 30,000 Tunisian migrant workers not only created hardships for these workers and their families but also served as a reminder for the Tunisian government about just how unpredictable their neighbor to the east was.

Tunisia's relations with Libya have been complicated by economic issues. The two countries had competing claims for an oil-rich section of the Gulf of Gabès, oil resources that could be very important to the Tunisian economy. The International Court of Justice at the Hague favored Libya in the settlement of this dispute.

In recent years, Qaddafi and President Ben Ali have eased tensions between their two countries. The leaders have initiated dialogue about economic cooperation.

RELATIONS WITH ALGERIA

Historically, Tunisia has had a more intimate, albeit frequently tense, relationship with its neighbor to the west, Algeria. During Algeria's war for independence from France in the 1950s, Tunisia tried to mediate between the two parties. It also provided a base from which Algerian rebel leaders could operate. At the same time, Tunisia needed to maintain friendly relations with France because it was still somewhat dependent on France economically in the early years of its statehood.

Even after the end of Algeria's civil war, Tunisia's friendly relationship with France remained a source of tension between the two

Maghreb countries. In 1970, however, Tunisia and Algeria resolved a dispute about their mutual border that had existed since the civil war. They also concluded a treaty of friendship.

Since 1980 Tunisia and Algeria have worked together to create a cordial political and economic relationship, leading to a joint security treaty in 1983. Of all the countries in the Maghreb, Algeria and Tunisia probably share the closest ties today. Tunisia has watched with great concern the unfolding of the bitter, violent conflict during the 1990s between the Algerian regime and Islamist opposition groups.

TUNISIA'S PLACE IN THE ARAB WORLD

Traditionally, the countries of the Maghreb and the Mashriq, the eastern part of the Arab world, have shared the Islamic faith. Yet these two regions have been divided by geographical distance and cultural attitudes. As a result, Tunisia's ties to the Arab world as a whole have not been as strong as its ties to the Maghreb. Even so, Tunisia has shared many of the concerns of the Arab world. Tunisia has supported efforts to resolve the Arab-Israeli conflict, including the U.S.-initiated diplomatic process in the 1990s.

Following independence, Tunisian foreign policy was wary of calls for Arab or Islamic unity, emphasizing instead the centrality of Tunisian nationalism. Tunisia did not join the Arab League right away, delaying its membership until 1958. Even then, it boycotted meetings until 1961 because of differences with the Egyptian leader, Gamal Abdel Nasser. Nasser, who dominated the Arab League from the mid-1950s until his death in 1970, sought to bring the Arab world under his, and Egypt's, influence, evoking the distrust of Bourguiba and other pro-Western Arab leaders. Since that time, Tunisia has kept its distance from more radical Arab states, such as Syria. In general, Tunisia has allied itself with the conservative, pro-Western Arab oil states, such as Saudi Arabia.

Foreign ministers from Tunisia, Jordan, Syria, Egypt, Saudi Arabia, Morocco, and Bahrain attend a two-day Arab League meeting in Amman, Jordan. Although Tunisia is a member of the Arab League, its moderate approach to foreign policy has at times set it apart from other members.

An important aspect of Tunisia's image in the eyes of the outside world has been its moderate views on the Arab-Israeli conflict. This position kept Tunisia on the sidelines in the Arab world for many years because it was at odds with the views of the majority of Arab states. However, by the 1970s, those views came to be more accepted among members of the Arab League, and Tunisia became more comfortable in the organization.

For many years, Cairo had been the home of the Arab League. But in 1978–79, Egypt was expelled from the league because of its unilateral peace treaty with Israel. As a result, Tunis became the new headquarters of the Arab League. A Tunisian, Chadli Klibi, was appointed secretary-general of the Arab League for two consecutive terms. During this period, Tunisia developed stronger relations with the Arab world. In agreement with other Arab nations, Tunisia strongly criticized Israel's invasion of Lebanon in 1982. At the same time, in a rare moment of disagreement with the West, it also criticized the United States for supplying military aid to Israel, which had made the attack possible.

Tunisia during the 1980s became further entangled in the Arab-Israeli conflict. In 1982 the Palestine Liberation Organization was forced to leave its main base of operations in Lebanon. Tunisia then volunteered to host the PLO leadership, and thus became home to more than 500 PLO members and their families. While Bourguiba's government was a generous host to the PLO, it was careful to keep the PLO apart from its own population. In 1985 Israeli warplanes raided PLO headquarters in Hamman-Lif, a suburb of Tunis. The

A group of young Palestinian guerrillas in the hills outside Tunis. After leaving Lebanon in 1982, the Palestine Liberation Organization (PLO) moved its headquarters to Tunisia.

raid, which killed at least 20 Tunisians and 80 Palestinians, raised concerns about Tunisian security. Most of the PLO contingent left Tunis after the signing of Palestinian-Israeli agreements in 1993–94.

RELATIONS WITH THE WEST

Tunisia has worked to establish plans for its own economic development with the oil states from the Persian Gulf. Loans from these countries—Saudi Arabia in particular—have been vital to strengthening Tunisia's economy, especially with regard to developing industry and tourism in recent years.

Under Bourguiba, Tunisia usually allied itself with the West. President Ben Ali has continued to cultivate strong ties to the West and to the United States in particular, in order to encourage foreign investment. In the past, much of Tunisia's foreign aid came from the United States. Ties to the United States go back two centuries, to 1797, when the first American consul arrived in Tunis. The United States was the first foreign country to recognize Tunisia's independence in 1956. For many years, the United States has supported Tunisia, appreciating Tunisia's moderate voice in debates in the Arab world even though the Tunisian government has occasionally been critical of U.S. support of Israel. After France, the United States is the largest market for Tunisian products.

Ties to France have also been highly important to Tunisia, not only because of the two nations' shared history but also because Bourguiba was determined to keep Tunisia's French heritage a part of his country's culture after independence. However, there have been times when this relationship was strained. In 1964 Tunisia nationalized all French-owned property, and France cancelled all aid to Tunisia. Disputes with France were resolved in the 1970s, and since that time, France has been a primary trade partner and the main source of tourism to Tunisia.

Tunisia's Mediterranean heritage and relatively benign colonial experience have given it a more pro-European outlook than other Arab states. It maintains cordial relations with European nations, and since 1969 Tunisia has been associated with the European Economic Community and its successor, the European Union (EU). However, the imbalance in trade has remained an issue. EU countries tend to export high-value manufactured products to Tunisia, while Tunisia exports lower-value raw materials and agricultural products to Europe. The trade deficit with European countries is offset, to some degree, by the remittances from Tunisian workers in European countries.

TUNISIA AND AFRICA

Tunisia is an active member of the major organizations in the Arab, Muslim, and African worlds. It is part of the Arab League and the Organization of the Islamic Conference. It was a founding member, in 1963, of the Organization of African Unity. President Ben Ali has worked to strengthen ties with southern Africa and is committed to negotiating solutions to the various armed conflicts occurring in Africa.

In spite of its relatively small size, Tunisia has used its tradition of stability and cultural strength to influence its corner of the global community.

CHRONOLOGY

Ca. 1100 B.C.:   Coastal areas in what is now Tunisia are settled by Phoenicians from Tyre, in what is now Lebanon.

814 B.C.:   Carthage, which will become a powerful city-state, is founded.

264–146 B.C.:   Rome and Carthage fight three wars called the Punic Wars; Rome ultimately triumphs, destroying Carthage in 146.

1st century B.C.:   Large-scale Roman colonization of North Africa begins.

A.D. 439:   Carthage is conquered by the Vandals.

533: Carthage is made part of the Byzantine Empire.

670: Islamic army establishes Kairouan as a holy city and outpost for further conquest.

698: Arabs take Carthage; Tunisia comes under the control of the first Arab caliphate.

800–909:   Expansion of Islam; foundation of the Aghlabid dynasty.

909–1159:   Fatamid and Zirid dynasties.

921: Foundation of the city of Mahdia.

1159–1250: Almohad dynasty rules over region of Maghreb and southern Spain.

1230–1574: Rule of Berber Hafsid dynasty; capital is moved to Tunis.

1574: Tunisia is conquered by the Ottoman Empire.

Ca. 1820:   Significant European influence in Tunisia begins.

1881: Tunisia becomes a French protectorate.

1907: The Young Tunisians political party forms in Tunis.

1914: Tunisians fight alongside the French army in Europe during World War I.

1920: The Destour (Constitution) Party is formed.

1933: Habib Bourguiba and other young nationalists form the Neo-Destour Party.

1942: Germany invades Tunisia in World War II.

1949: Bourguiba is imprisoned for political activities.

1954: French government begins negotiations with Tunisians for independence.

1956: Tunisia gains its independence.

1957: Tunisia becomes a republic, with Habib Bourguiba as president.

CHRONOLOGY

1959: Tunisia's new constitution is put in place.

1961: French evacuate Bizerte, their last stronghold in Tunisia.

1975: Bourguiba is elected president-for-life.

1978–79: Tunisia becomes the host country for the Arab League, following the expulsion of Egypt.

1981: Political parties other than the ruling party become legal.

1982: Tunisia becomes the host country for the Palestine Liberation Organization.

1984: During anti-government riots in southern Tunisia, 89 people are killed and many more are wounded.

1987: General Zine El Abidine Ben Ali deposes Bourguiba, on the grounds of senility.

1989: Tunisia joins the Arab Maghreb Union; after relatively competitive parliamentary elections, during which candidates backed by the Islamist Al-Nahda party win 14 percent of the vote, the regime outlaws the organization.

1994: The government arrests political dissidents during elections.

1995: Tunisia signs free trade agreement with the European Union.

1999: Ben Ali is reelected with nearly 100 percent of the vote, after running against two token candidates from opposition parties.

2001: Ben Ali announces reforms to the constitution incorporating human-rights protections.

2002: Islamist terrorist group al-Qaeda bombs Jewish synagogues in Tunis and on Jerba Island.

2003: El Abidine Mosque is opened in Carthage, north of Tunis, with room for 1,000 worshippers.

2004: President Zine El Abidine Ben Ali is reelected with 94 percent of the vote. Opposition leaders dispute the official results.

2005: Israeli prime minister Ariel Sharon invited to visit Tunis amid protests from Tunisian opposition parties.

2007: In Tunis, 12 members of an Islamist group die in a clash with security forces.

2008: A journalist who criticized the Tunisian government is released from prison amid nationwide controversy about free speech.

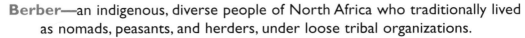

GLOSSARY

Berber—an indigenous, diverse people of North Africa who traditionally lived as nomads, peasants, and herders, under loose tribal organizations.

bey—a native ruler of Tunis or Tunisia during the Ottoman period; or, more generally, a governor of a province of the Ottoman Empire.

caliph—the religious and political leader of an Islamic empire.

colon—a French colonist; also, any European living in a French colony.

elite—the privileged, ruling class of society.

gourbiville—a shantytown, or slum, ringing a Tunisian city.

gross domestic product (GDP)—the total value of goods and services produced in a country in a one-year period.

Hadith—the collected sayings of the prophet Muhammad.

Islamist—a political group or individual motivated by the ideals of fundamentalist Islam.

madrasa—a school for the teaching of Islam, usually associated with a mosque.

Maghreb—the northwestern African countries of Tunisia, Algeria, and Morocco, as well as, on occasion, Libya and Mauritania.

medina—the old Arabic residential district of a North African city.

mercenary—a professional soldier who fights strictly for pay.

Moorish—the culture of the North African Arabs and Berbers who ruled North Africa and parts of Spain from the 8th to the 15th centuries.

nomadic—having no permanent home but moving from place to place in search of food and water.

notables—members of the upper class of Tunisian (and most Arab) societies; Tunisian notables are often families who trace their ancestry back to the leaders of the Arab armies who first conquered the country beginning in the late seventh century.

Phoenicians—a Semitic-speaking people, with origins in what is now Lebanon, who were important in the Mediterranean region from about 1100 to 625 B.C. as merchants and colonizers.

protectorate—a state protected or controlled by another, more powerful, state.

Punic—of or relating to the people or culture of ancient Carthage.

GLOSSARY

Sahel—the region in eastern Tunisia that is formed by the low-lying westward extension of the coastal plain.

Sharia—Islamic law.

socialism—a political system in which the state owns and distributes the goods and services of agriculture and industry.

umma—the worldwide community of Muslim believers.

Western—referring to countries and cultures of Europe or North America.

FURTHER READING

Brown, Rosalind Varghese. *Tunisia.* 2nd ed. New York: Benchmark Books, 2008.

Charrad, Mourina M. *States and Women's Rights: The Making of Postcolonial Tunisia, Algeria, and Morocco.* Los Angeles: University of California Press, 2001.

Fox, Mary Virginia. *Tunisia.* New York: Scholastic, 1994.

Henry, Clement M. *The Mediterranean Debt Crescent: Money and Power in Algeria, Egypt, Morocco, Tunisia, and Turkey.* Gainesville: University Press of Florida, 1996.

Hole, Abigail, et al. *Tunisia.* 4th ed. Oakland, Calif.: Lonely Planet Publications, 2007.

Kelly, Orr. *Meeting the Fox: The Allied Invasion of Africa, from Operation Torch to Kasserine Pass to Victory in Tunisia.* New York: John Wiley and Sons, 2002.

Perkins, Kenneth J. *Historical Dictionary of Tunisia.* Lanham, Md.: Scarecrow Press, 1997.

Seguin, Yves, and Marie-Josee Guy. *Tunisia.* Montreal: Ulysses Travel Publishing, 2000.

White, Gregory. *A Comparative Political Economy of Tunisia and Morocco.* Albany: State University of New York Press, 2001.

Zarr, Gerald. *Tunisia: A Quick Guide to Customs and Culture.* London: Kuperard Publishers, 2009.

Zartman, I. William, ed. *Tunisia: The Political Economy of Reform.* Boulder, Colo.: Lynne Rienner Publishing, 1991.

INTERNET RESOURCES

http://www.tunisiaonline.com

This website has great images in the following categories: history, environment, society, women, political life, economy, culture, tourism, news, sports, media, and mosaics.

http://www.sesrtcic.org/member_countries.php

The website of the Statistical, Economic and Social Research and Training Centre for Islamic Countries has statistical information about the economy and demographics of Tunisia.

http://www.hejleh.com/countries/tunisia.html

Includes a narrative history of Tunisia as well as an exhaustive list of links to other sites, including links to many Tunisian cities and towns.

http://www.cia.gov/cia/libary/publications/the-world-factbook/geos/ts.html

Includes demographic and economic statistics as well as political information.

http://www.mideastinfo.com/

Includes links to government, politics, education, news and media, and a list of other online resources for the nations of the Middle East.

INDEX

Numbers in **bold italic** refer to captions.

INDEX

INDEX

CONTRIBUTORS

The **FOREIGN POLICY RESEARCH INSTITUTE (FPRI)** served as editorial consultants for the MAJOR MUSLIM NATIONS series. FPRI is one of the nation's oldest "think tanks." The Institute's Middle East Program focuses on Gulf security, monitors the Arab-Israeli peace process, and sponsors an annual conference for teachers on the Middle East, plus periodic briefings on key developments in the region.

Among the FPRI's trustees is a former Secretary of State and a former Secretary of the Navy (and among the FPRI's former trustees and interns, two current Undersecretaries of Defense), not to mention two university presidents emeritus, a foundation president, and several active or retired corporate CEOs.

The scholars of FPRI include a former aide to three U.S. Secretaries of State, a Pulitzer Prize–winning historian, a former president of Swarthmore College and a Bancroft Prize–winning historian, and two former staff members of the National Security Council. And the FPRI counts among its extended network of scholars—especially, its Inter-University Study Groups—representatives of diverse disciplines, including political science, history, economics, law, management, religion, sociology, and psychology.

DR. HARVEY SICHERMAN is president and director of the Foreign Policy Research Institute in Philadelphia, Pennsylvania. He has extensive experience in writing, research, and analysis of U.S. foreign and national security policy, both in government and out. He served as Special Assistant to Secretary of State Alexander M. Haig Jr. and as a member of the Policy Planning Staff of Secretary of State James A. Baker III. Dr. Sicherman was also a consultant to Secretary of the Navy John F. Lehman Jr. (1982–1987) and Secretary of State George Shultz (1988).

A graduate of the University of Scranton (B.S., History, 1966), Dr. Sicherman earned his Ph.D. at the University of Pennsylvania (Political Science, 1971), where he received a Salvatori Fellowship. He is author or editor of numerous books and articles, including *America the Vulnerable: Our Military Problems and How to Fix Them* (FPRI, 2002) and *Palestinian Autonomy, Self-Government and Peace* (Westview Press, 1993). He edits *Peacefacts*, an FPRI bulletin that monitors the Arab-Israeli peace process.

ANNA CAREW-MILLER is a professor of English at Teikyo Post University. She is the author of several works of nonfiction for younger audiences and writes frequently about the natural world and the environment. She lives in rural Connecticut with her family.